The ⎯ of ⎯

Its Origin, Meaning and Privileges

From the French of the
**Right Rev. Dom. Prosper Guéranger, O.S.B.
Abbot of Solesmes.**

*Edited, with an introduction, and an appendix
on the Centenary Medal, etc., by a Monk
of the English Benedictine Congregation of
St. Edmond's College, Douai, France.*

"God forbid that I should glory, save in the cross of our Lord Jesus Christ"
— *Gal. vi.14.*

"It is right and just, O Eternal God, to beseech thy Majesty, with many prayers, that, assisted by the protection of St. Benedict, we may give glory to thy name by our dutiful service." — *Gerbert, O.S.B.*

Loreto Publications
P.O. Box 603
Fitzwilliam, NH 03447
www.loretopubs.org

First Published by:
Burns and Oates,
London, 1880

Published by:
Loreto Publications
P.O. Box 603
Fitzwilliam, NH, 03447
www.loretopubs.org

ISBN 1-930278-21-7
Printed and Bound in the USA
All Rights Reserved

Tenth Printing	:	April, 2002
Eleventh Printing	:	November, 2005
Twelfth Printing	:	November, 2007
Fourteenth Printing		March 2016

To
The Benedictine Saints of England;
and to their Brethren of the
present day, working in the quiet
of the Cloister like St. Bede,
or in the turmoil of the Mission
like St. Boniface; this little work on
St. Benedict and his cross
is humbly and reverently dedicated.

CONTENTS

INTRODUCTION

The original of this *translation* was written by the venerable restorer of the Benedictines in France, to propagate a devotion which had already become very popular in Italy and Germany. It is now brought out in an English form, in the hope that it may be the means of making the name of St. Benedict better known, and of spreading devotion to him in this age, which seems specially to need his spirit.

The following account of St. Benedict's mission and life is extracted from Abbot Guéranger's "Liturgical Year."[1]

With what profound veneration ought we not to celebrate the name of this wonderful Saint, who as St. Gregory says, "was filled with the spirit of all the just!" If we consider his virtues, we find nothing superior in the annals of perfection presented to our admiration by the Church. Love of God and man, humility, the gift of prayer, dominion over the passions, form him into a masterpiece of the grace of the Holy Ghost. Miracles seem to constitute his life; he cures the sick, commands the elements, casts out devils, and raises

---

[1] See English Translation. Lent, March 21st

the dead to life. The spirit of prophecy unfolds futurity to him; and the most intimate thoughts of men are not too distant for the eye of his mind to scan. These superhuman qualifications are heightened by a sweet majesty, a serene gravity, and a tender charity, which shine in every page of his wonderful life; it is one of his holiest children who wrote it — St. Gregory the Great. It is this holy Pope and doctor who had the honor of telling posterity all the wonders which God vouchsafed to work in His servant Benedict.

Yes, posterity had a right to know the life and virtues of a man whose salutary influence upon the Church and society has been so observable during the ages of the Christian era. To describe the influence exercised by the spirit of St. Benedict, we should have to transcribe the annals of all the nations of the Western Church, from the seventh century down to our own times. Benedict is the Father of Europe. By his Benedictines, numerous as the stars of heaven, and as the sands of the sea-shore, he rescued the last remnants of Roman vigor from the total annihilation threatened by the invasion of barbarians; he presided over the establishment of the public and private laws of those nations which grew out of the ruins of the Roman Empire; he carried the Gospel and civilization into England, Germany, and the northern countries, including Sclavonia; and to conclude, he saved the precious deposit of the arts and sciences from the tempest which would have swept them from the world and would have left mankind a prey to a gloomy and fatal ignorance.

And Benedict did all this by that little book which we

call his "Rule." This admirable code of Christian perfection and prudence disciplined the countless legions of religious by whom the holy Patriarch achieved all these prodigies. During the ages which preceded the promulgation of this "Rule"— so wonderful in its simple eloquence — the monastic life in the Western Church had produced some few saintly men, but there was nothing to justify the hope that this kind of life would become, even *more* than it had been in the East, the principal means of the Christian regeneration and civilization of so many nations. But before this "Rule" all other rules, one by one, disappeared as the stars fade away when the sun rises. The West was peopled with monasteries, and from these monasteries flowed upon Europe all those blessings which have made it the privileged quarter of the globe.

An incredible number of saints, both men and women, who look up to Benedict as their Father, purify and sanctify the world, which had not yet emerged from the state of semi-barbarism. A long series of popes, who had once been novices in the Benedictine cloister, preside over the destinies of this new world, and form for it a new legislation, which, being based exclusively on the moral law, is to avert the threatening prevalence of brutal despotism. Bishops innumerable, trained in the same school of Benedict, consolidate this moral legislation in the provinces and cities over which they are appointed. The Apostles of twenty barbarous nations confront their fierce and savage tribes, and, with the Gospel in one hand, and the "Rule" of their Holy Father in the other, lead them into the fold of Christ.

For many centuries the learned men, the doctors of the Church, and the instructors of youth, belong, almost exclusively, to the Order of the Great Patriarch, who, by the labors of his children, pours forth on the people the purest beauty of light and truth. This choir of heroes in every virtue, of popes, of bishops, of apostles, of holy doctors, proclaiming themselves his disciples, and joining with the universal Church in glorifying that God Whose holiness and power shine forth so brightly in the life and actions of Benedict — what a *Corona,* what an aureola of glory for one saint to have!

St. Benedict was born[1] of a noble family at Nursia.[2] He was sent to Rome that he might receive a liberal education; but not long after he withdrew to a place called Subiaco, and there hid himself in a very deep cave, that he might give himself entirely to Jesus Christ. He passed three years in that retirement, unknown to all save to a monk, by name Romanus, who supplied him with the necessaries of life. The devil having one day excited him to a violent temptation of impurity, he rolled himself amidst prickly brambles and extinguished within himself the desire of carnal pleasure by the pain he thus endured. The fame of his sanctity, however, became known beyond the limits of his hiding-place, and certain monks put themselves under his guidance. He sharply rebuked them for their wicked lives: which rebuke so irritated them that they resolved to put poison in his drink. Having made the sign of the cross

[1] A.D. 480
[2] About fifty miles east of Rome, in the province of Umbria

over the cup as they proffered it to him, it broke, and, leaving that monastery, he returned to his solitude.

But whereas many daily came to him, beseeching him to take them as his disciples, he built twelve monasteries, and drew up the most admirable rules for their government. He afterwards went to Monte Cassino,[1] where he destroyed an image of Apollo, which was still adored in those parts; and having pulled down the altar and burned the groves, he built a chapel in that same place, in honor of St. Martin, and another in honor of St. John. He instructed the inhabitants in the Christian religion. Day by day did Benedict advance in the grace of God, so that he even foretold, in a spirit of prophecy, what was to take place. Totila, the King of the Goths, having heard of this, and being anxious to know if it were the truth, went to visit him; but first he sent his sword-bearer, who was to pretend that he was the king, and who, for this end, was dressed in royal robes and accompanied by a royal retinue. As soon as Benedict saw him, he said, "Put off, my son, put off this dress, for it is not thine." But he foretold to Totila that he would reach Rome, cross the sea, and die at the end of nine years.

Several months before he departed from this life, he foretold to his disciples the day on which he should die. Six days previous to his death he ordered them to open the sepulchre wherein he wished to be buried. On the sixth day he desired to be carried to the church; and there, having received the Eucharist, with his eyes raised in prayer towards heaven, and supported in the arms of his disciples, he

[1] Seventy miles south-west of Rome.

breathed forth his soul.[1] Two monks saw it ascending to heaven, adorned with a most precious robe, and surrounded by shining lights. They also saw a most beautiful and venerable man, who stood above the saint's head, and they heard him speak thus: "This is the way whereby Benedict, the beloved of the Lord, ascended to heaven."

There is an ancient tradition, which says that God revealed to St. Benedict that his Order should not disappear from the world's stage until the Last Day; and that, in the fierce times preceding the judgment, it should prove a support to the Church and strengthen many in the faith. Some think we have entered upon the last days. Certain it is that the sons of the holy patriarch are increasing in number and influence. Perhaps the reason is, that the evils of an age resembling in many points those times for which St. Benedict labored and prayed, call once more for the spirit and example of the great Patriarch.

There is no way more common of making known a saint, of inspiring the faithful with his spirit, and of drawing down his protection, than by medals bearing his effigy and struck in his honor. This method of preaching devotion to St. Benedict has been peculiarly successful in the Church for some centuries. God has blessed it by singular favors granted in the most varied circumstances of life, and in the most distant countries.

Moved by these tokens of Divine favor, the Church has approved of the medal of St. Benedict, and in the form of blessing prays God, by the intercession of St. Benedict,

[1] A.D. 543

to give those who wear it health of body and mind, to protect them from the frauds and snares of the demons, to grant them His grace and indulgence, to preserve them, amid the dangers of the times, stainless and pure in His sight, and through the sufferings of Jesus Christ to bring them safely to the heavenly country.

J B M.

ST. EDMUND'S, DOUAI,
Lent, 1880.

When using the Medal for any pious purpose,
the following prayer may be said:

May the intercession of the Blessed Patriarch and Abbot Benedict render Thee, O Lord, merciful unto us; that what our own unworthiness cannot obtain we may receive through his powerful patronage: Through Christ Our Lord.

AUTHOR'S PREFACE

Man has no right to pass judgment on the effects which God deigns to produce by His power and goodness. In order to assist us in our necessities, God, in His wisdom and providence, sometimes makes use of extremely simple means, thus to keep us in humility and filial confidence. A Christian whose faith is but weak, is surprised at this, and even tempted to be scandalized, inasmuch as it seems to him that the means by which God works are not in keeping with His greatness. Such a thought as this is nothing less than pride or ignorance, for whenever God puts Himself within our reach, He must needs stoop down to our lowliness.

And yet, does He not show His greatness when He selects simple material objects as the medium of communication between Himself and us, as in the case of the Holy Sacraments? Does He not thereby show us how He is the absolute Master of all, even so far as this — that He can embody his grace in such lowly and apparently commonplace forms as these? The Church, which is guided by His Spirit, delights in imitating this His mode of acting, at least in some slight way, and hence she communicates the divine virtue which she possesses to those objects which she sanctifies as helps and consolations for her children.

This little work treats of one of these sacred objects; one which is honored with the approbation and blessing of the Church, and which unites in itself the triumphant power of the holy cross which redeemed us, with the memory of one of God's most illustrious servants. Every Christian that loves and adores Christ Who redeemed us, or who believes in the intercession of the Saints who are now reigning in heaven with Him, will look on the medal of St. Benedict with respect; and when he hears of any of those heavenly favors of which it has been the instrument, he will give thanks to God, Who authorizes us to make use of His Son's cross as a shield of protection, and to rely with confidence on the assistance of the Saints in heaven.

We have collected together in these pages a certain number of facts which prove that God deigns to protect, in a special manner those who put their confidence in the sacred signs marked on the medal. These facts, to which we in no manner wish to attribute the name of *miracles* properly so called, have been told us by persons in whom we have the fullest confidence. The reader is at liberty to form his own judgment upon them, and believe them or not, as he pleases. Numerous as they are, we could easily have given very many more, of all of which we have received the particulars; but we thought it advisable to limit ourselves to those we have related, and to aim rather at variety than number.

In publishing this work upon a subject which to many may seem ill fitted for an age like this, when Rationalism is so rife, our only object is to render a service to our brethren in the faith. During life they will be placed in circumstances when they will feel that they need a special help from Heaven. Let them, at these times, have recourse to the medal of St. Benedict, as so many Christians are in the habit of doing; and if their faith be strong and simple, they may depend on the promise of our Lord — such faith shall not go unrewarded.

The Medal or Cross of St. Benedict

ITS ORIGIN, MEANING, AND PRIVILEGES

CHAPTER I

ON THE FIGURE OF THE CROSS
REPRESENTED ON THE MEDAL

There is a great wish on the part of many Catholics to have clear ideas regarding the celebrated medal, which goes under the name of the great Patriarch of the Monks of the West. It is true that several notices, some more, some less correct, have been already published; but not one of them — so it seems to us — having fully satisfied the wishes of the faithful, we thought it would be well to offer to their devotion a more complete explanation of an object, which has become so dear to them. That there may be order in what we are going to say about it, we will begin with the description of the medal.

A Christian needs but reflect for a moment on the sovereign virtue of the cross of Jesus Christ, in order to understand how worthy of respect a medal is on which it is represented. The cross was the instrument of the world's redemption; it is the saving tree whereon was expiated the sin committed by man, when he ate the fruit of the forbidden tree. St. Paul tells us that the sentence of our condemnation was fastened to the cross, and blotted out by the blood of our Redeemer. In a word, the cross, which the Church, salutes as *our only hope, "Spes Unica,"* is to appear at the last day in the clouds of heaven as the trophy of the victory of the Man-God.

The image of the cross excites in our minds the liveliest sentiments of gratitude towards God for the benefit of our salvation. After the Blessed Sacrament, there is nothing on earth so deserving our respect as the cross; and it is for this reason that we pay it a worship of adoration which is referred to God, whose precious blood was spilt upon it.

Animated by sentiments of the purest religion, the primitive Christians had, from the very beginning of the Church, the profoundest veneration for the image of the cross, and the Fathers seem never to tire in the praises they give to this august sign. When, after three hundred years of persecution, God had decreed to give peace to His Church, there appeared in the heavens a cross, on which were these words, "In this sign shalt thou conquer;" and the Emperor Constantine, to whom was granted this vision, promising him victory over his enemies, would henceforth have his army go to battle under a standard bearing the image of the cross with the monogram of the word "Christ." This standard was called the *Labarum.*

The cross is an object of terror to the evil spirits; they ever crouch in terror before it; they no sooner see it than they let go their prey and take to flight. In a word, of such importance to Christians is the cross and the blessing it brings along with it, that from the times of the Apostles, down to our own age, the faithful have ever been accustomed frequently to make the sign of the cross upon themselves, and the priests of the Church have constantly used it over all the objects which, in virtue of their sacerdotal character, they have the power to bless and sanctify.

Our medal, therefore, which firstly offers to us the figure of the cross, is in strict accordance with Christian piety, and worthy, even were there no other motive than this, of all possible veneration.

CHAPTER II

OF THE EFFIGY OF ST. BENEDICT
REPRESENTED ON THE MEDAL

The honor of appearing on the same medal with the figure of the holy cross has been given to St. Benedict, with the intention of expressing the efficacy which this holy sign had, when made by his venerable hand. St. Gregory the Great, who has written the Life of the holy Patriarch, tells us how, by the sign of the cross, he overcame his temptations, and by the same sign broke the cup of poisoned drink which was proffered to him, thus unmasking the wicked designs of those who had plotted to take away his life. When the evil spirit, in order to terrify his Religious, made the monastery of Monte Cassino appear to be on fire, St. Benedict immediately dispels the artifice by making over the fiery phantom this same sign of our Redeemer's Passion.[1] When his Religious are troubled interiorly with the suggestions of the tempter, the Holy Father bids them take the remedy, and it is to make on their breasts the sign of the cross.[2]

[1] See his Life, chap. x.   [2] Ibid., chap. xx.

In his Rule, he prescribes that the brother, who has been reading the solemn engagement of his profession at the foot of the altar, should immediately affix to it the sign of the cross, as an irrevocable seal of the deed on which his vows are written.

The disciples of St. Benedict have had a like confidence in this sacred sign, and have worked innumerable miracles by it. Let it here suffice to mention St. Maurus giving sight to a blind man; St. Placid curing many who were sick; St. Richmir liberating captives; St. Wulstan preserving a workman in the very act of falling from the top of the church-tower; St. Odilo drawing out from a man's eye a splinter of wood which had run through it; St. Anselm of Canterbury driving away from an old man the horrid spectres which were tormenting him in his dying moments; St. Hugh of Cluny quelling a storm; St. Gregory the Seventh arresting the conflagration at Rome, etc.: these, and a thousand other such miracles, which are related in the "Acts of the Saints of the Order of St. Benedict," were all worked by the sign of the cross.

The glory and efficacy of the august instrument of our salvation have been celebrated with enthusiasm by the children of the great Patriarch; they loved to extol it, for their hearts were full of gratitude towards it. Not to speak of the little Office of the Holy Cross which St. Udalric, Bishop of Augsburg, used to recite, and which was also said in choir in the abbeys of St. Gall, of Reichenau, of Bursfeld, etc.; the blessed Rhabanus Maurus and St. Peter Damian consecrated their talent for poetry in singing the praises of the holy cross; St. Anselm of Canterbury has written its praises in the form of most exquisite prayers; Venerable Bede, St. Odilo of Cluny, Rupert of Deutz, Ecbert of Schonaugen, and a long list of others of the Order, have left us sermons on the holy cross; Eginhard wrote a book in defence of the worship paid to it against the Iconoclasts, and Peter the Venerable defended, in a set treatise, the use of the sign of the cross, which had been attacked by the Petrobrusians. A great number of the most famous monasteries of the Order of St. Benedict were founded under the title of "Holy Cross." Of these, let it suffice to mention the celebrated monastery built at Paris by the Bishop, St. Germanus; the monastery built by St. Faron in the diocese of Meaux; the abbey of "Holy Cross" founded at Poitiers by St. Radegonde; the monastery of "Holy Cross" at Bordeaux built by Clovis the Second; those of Metten in Bavaria, Reichenau in Switzerland, Quimperle in Brittany, and the five famous monasteries in the Vosgian country which were founded by St. Hydulph, and which he so situated that they formed a cross.

The Savior of the world seems to have entrusted, by a special favor, to the children of St. Benedict a large portion of the cross on which He died for the redemption of man. Large fragments of this sacred wood have been confided to their keeping, and a Christian might almost glory in having seen the instrument of his salvation, were all the pieces to be put before him, which have been possessed by different monasteries of this Order. We may mention the following amongst the houses thus privileged: In

France, St. Germain-des-Pres, in Paris, St. Denis'; Holy Cross at Poitiers; Cormery, in Touraine, Gellone, etc.; St. Michael's de Murano, in Venice; Sahagun, in Spain; Reichenau, in Switzerland; St. Ulric's and St. Afra's at Augsburg, in Germany; St. Michael's, at Hildesheim; St. Trutpert's, in the Black Forest; Mœlk, in Austria; the celebrated monastery of Gandersheim, etc.

But the most glorious mission given to the Benedictines in what relates to the glory of the Holy Cross is that of having carried this instrument of salvation into so many countries by preaching the gospel to their pagan inhabitants. The greater part of the West was converted by their zeal from the darkness of infidelity; and the reader need scarce be told that England was converted by St. Augustine of Canterbury; Germany by St. Boniface; Belgium by St. Amandus; Holland and Zealand by St. Willibrord; Westphalia by St. Swithbert; Sweden and Denmark by St. Anscharius; Austria by St. Wolfgang; Saxony by St. Ludgerius; Bavaria by St. Corbinian; Poland and Bohemia by St. Adalbert of Prague; Prussia by St. Otho of Bamberg; Russia by St. Boniface the Second.

Such are, in brief, the facts which give to the person and name of St. Benedict a special connection with the Holy Cross; it is, therefore, with a most evident appropriateness that the effigy of this holy Patriarch has been put on the same medal with the figure of the cross of our Lord Jesus Christ.

We see still more clearly why this should have been done when we refer to what is related in the Acts of the two great disciples of this servant of God, St. Placid and St. Maurus. Both of them, when working the miracles, which we meet with in almost every page of their lives, were wont to join together with the invocation of the Holy Cross the name of their holy Father, Benedict, thus establishing, at the very beginning of the Order, the pious practice, of which the medal was to be, in after times, the symbol and the expression.

St. Placid had scarcely bidden farewell to the holy Patriarch on leaving Monte Cassino to repair to Sicily, when arriving at Capua he was besought to heal the dean of the church of that town. His humility made him for a long time resist such a demand; at length he consents, and placing his hand upon the head of the priest, who was sick of a mortal disease, he immediately cures him, whilst pronouncing these words: "In the name of our Lord Jesus Christ, Who, *by the prayers and Virtue of Benedict our Master,* drew me safe and sound from the midst of the water, may God reward thy faith, and restore thee to thy former health."

Immediately there comes a blind man, begging in his turn to be cured. Placid makes the sign of the cross upon his eyes, at the same time adding this prayer: "Lord Jesus Christ, Mediator of God and men, Who didst come down from heaven to earth that Thou mightest enlighten those who were sitting in the darkness and shades of death; Thou Who hast given to our blessed Master Benedict the gift of healing all maladies and all wounds, deign, by his merits, to give sight to this blind man, to the end that, seeing the magnificence of Thy works, he may fear and

adore thee as the Sovereign Lord." Then addressing himself
to the blind man, Placid thus continued: "By the merits
of our most holy Father Benedict, I command thee, in the
name of Him Who created the sun and moon to be the
ornament of the heavens, and gave to him who was born
blind the eyes which nature had denied him, arise, and
be thou healed! Go now and tell all men the wonderful
works of our God." The blind man immediately recovered
his sight. We might quote several other miracles from the
life of St. Placid, such as healing the sick or driving out
devils from those possessed, in which the invocation or
the mention of St. Benedict, still living, was united with
the making of the sign of the cross. In some of these
miracles, we find the sick themselves acknowledging and
proclaiming this mysterious connection.

St. Maurus, having been sent by the great Patriarch into
Gaul, there to establish his Rule, soon began to work
numerous miracles. As we noticed before, these miracles
were wrought by means of the Holy Cross, but the saintly
abbot was also accustomed to join to the divine virtue of
the instrument of our redemption a prayer invoking the
intervention of St. Benedict. He bore testimony to this
himself when, on occasion of his having saved one of his
fellow-travelers from death, he made this declaration: "If,"
said the saint to those who had witnessed the miracle, "the
Divine Majesty hath deigned to work this miracle by the
wood which redeemed us, it is plainly not to man, but to
the Redeemer Himself that we must give the glory of it,
although none of you can doubt, but that *the merits of our*

most holy Father Benedict have obtained this grace of Him for us."

From these facts it is evident that even from the very commencement of the Benedictine Order, this method of having recourse to the divine goodness was practised with wonderful success. St. Benedict was still on earth, and his disciples invoked his name when they were asking favors of Heaven; if such confidence in his merits was, even then, thus blessed by God, how great must the power of his intercession be now that he has been raised to his throne of glory in heaven!

CHAPTER III

Besides the two figures of the cross and of St. Benedict, there are also inscribed on the medal a certain number of letters, each of which is the initial of a Latin word. These words compose one or two sentences, which explain the medal and its object. They express the relation existing between the holy Patriarch of the Monks of the West and the sacred sign of the salvation of mankind, at the same time that they offer the faithful a formula, which they may make use of, for employing the virtue of the Holy Cross against the evil spirits.

These mysterious letters are arranged on that side of the medal on which the cross is. Let us begin by noticing the four which are placed in the angles formed by the arms of the cross.

C.	**S.**
P.	**B.**

They signify: CRUX SANCTI PATRIS BENEDICTI; in English:

The Cross of Holy Father Benedict. These words explain the nature of the medal.

On the perpendicular line of the cross itself are these letters:

C.

S.

S.

M.

L.

They stand for these words: CRUX SACRA SIT MIHI LUX; in English: *May the Holy Cross be my Light.*

On the horizontal line of the cross are these letters:-

N. D. S. M. D.

The words which they imply are: NON DRACO SIT MIHI DUX; in English: *Let not the Dragon be my Guide.*

These two lines put together form a pentameter verse, containing the Christian's protestation that he confides in the Holy Cross, and refuses to bear the yoke which the devil would put upon him.

On the rim of the medal there are inscribed several other letters; and first the well-known monogram of the Holy Name of Jesus, I. H. S.[1] Faith and our own experience convince us of the all-powerfulness of this Divine name. Then follow, beginning at the right hand the following letters:

---

[1] The Holy Name in Greek is ΙΗΣΟΥΣ. ΙΗΣ are the first three letters of this word. As Jesus signifies Saviour, the three letters, without great departure from the truth, easily came to be explained as the initial letters of the phrase, Jesu Hominum Salvator. —Ed.

V. R. S. N. S. M. V. S. M. Q. L. I. V. B.

These initials stand for the two following verses:

VADE RETRO, SATANA; NUNQUAM SUADE MIHI VANA.
SUNT MALA QUÆ LIBAS; IPSE VENENA BIBAS;

in English: *Begone, Satan! and suggest not to me thy vain things: the cup thou profferest me is evil; drink thou thy poison.*

These words are supposed to be uttered by St. Benedict; those of the first verse when he was suffering the temptation in his cave,[1] and which he overcame by the sign of the cross; and those of the second verse, at the moment of his enemies offering him the draught of death, which he discovered by his making over the poisoned cup the sign of life.[2]

The Christian may make use of these same words as often as he finds himself tormented by the temptations and insults of the invisible enemy of our salvation. Our Savior sanctified the first of these words by Himself making use of them: "Begone, Satan!" *Vade retro, Satana.* Their efficacy has thus been tested, and the very Gospel is the guarantee of their power. *The vain things* to which the devil incites us are disobedience to the law of God; they are also the pomps and false maxims of the world. The *cup proffered* us by this angel of darkness is *evil,* that is, *sin,* which brings

---

[1] See Life of St. Benedict, chap. ii.   [2] Ibid., chap. iii

death to the soul. Instead of receiving it at his hands, we ought to bid him keep it to himself, for it is the inheritance which he chose for himself.

The Christian who reads these pages needs not that we should enter into a long explanation of this formula, which meets the artifices and violence of Satan with what he most dreads, namely, the cross, the holy name of Jesus, our Savior's own words in his temptation, and lastly, the mention of the victories which the great Patriarch St. Benedict gained over the infernal dragon. We need only pronounce these words of the medal with faith, and we shall immediately feel ourselves strengthened and encouraged to resist all that hell can do against us. Even did we know none of the countless facts which show us how strangely Satan fears this medal, the mere knowledge of what it means and what it expresses would be sufficient to make us look upon it as one of the most powerful arms which the goodness of God has put into our hands against the malice of the devils.

CHAPTER IV

ORIGIN OF THE MEDAL OF ST. BENEDICT

It would be impossible to say at what precise period the faithful began to make use of the medal which we have just described;[1] all we can do is to state the circumstances which caused it to become so widely spread in the Church, and elicited for it the express approbation of the Holy See.

In the year 1647, at Nattremberg in Bavaria, certain witches, who were accused of having exercised their spells to the injury of the people of the neighborhood, were put into prison by the authorities. In the examination which they were put to at their trial, they confessed that their superstitious practices had never been able to produce any effect wherever there was an image of the Holy Cross, either hung up or hidden underground. They added that they had never been able to

[1] It is a mistake to understand, as some have done, this verse of the hymn on St. Benedict, composed by Paul the Deacon, *Æther pluit numismata,* as expressing a much higher antiquity for our medal than we have mentioned in the text. These words are nothing more than an allusion to the miracle related by St. Gregory the Great in the Life of St. Benedict, chap. xxvii.

exercise any power over the monastery of Metten, and this circumstance had made them feel sure that the house was protected by the cross. The magistrates questioned the Benedictine monks of Metten upon this subject. Search was made in the monastery, and their attention was at length fixed upon several representations of the Holy Cross painted on the walls, and together with the cross were found the letters which we have been describing. These paintings were very ancient, but for years they had been passed by without notice. How, then, were the letters to be explained? No one in the house knew what they meant, and yet they alone could explain the reason of these crosses having been painted in this particular manner.

After many previous researches, they came to examine a manuscript belonging to the library of the monastery. It was an Evangeliarium or book of the Gospels, remarkable for its binding, which was inlaid with relics and precious stones. On the first page were written thirteen verses, telling the reader that this book was written and thus ornamented by order of Abbot Peter in the year 1415. At the end of this manuscript there was the book of Rabanus Maurus, *On the Cross,* and several pen-and-ink drawings made by one of the monks of Metten, who had concealed his name. One of these drawings represented St. Benedict in a monk's cowl, and holding in his right hand a staff, the end of which was formed into a cross. On the staff was written this verse:

CRUX SACRA SIT M. LUX.   N. DRACO SIT MICHI DUX.

The holy Patriarch was holding in his left hand a banner, on which were inscribed these two other lines:

VADE RETRO SATHANA NUQ. SUADE M. VANA.
SUNT MALA QUE LIBAS IPSE VENENA BIBAS.[1]

So that at the beginning of the fifteenth century, St. Benedict was represented holding a cross, and the verses the initials of which are now found on the medal, were known even at that time. These verses must have been at this period regarded as an object of special devotion, since the painting of the cross on the walls of the Metten monastery was encircled with their initial letters. At the same time, it is evident that the reason of these crosses having been placed on the walls had been lost sight of, and that the rich *Evangeliarium,* which we have just described from Dom Bernard Pez, had been almost forgotten, until an unexpected circumstance induced the monks to search in it for an explanation of the mysterious letters. We cannot be surprised at this carelessness, if we remember the vicissitudes through which the monasteries of Germany had passed for upwards of a century, owing to the religious and political disturbances, which had taken place in that country, and which had caused the suppression of so many of the monasteries,

---

[1] The description of the Metten manuscript was published in the year 1721, by the learned Dom Bernard Pez in the first volume of his "Thesaurus Anecdotorum Novissimus," in which he has given an engraving of the drawing in question.

leaving the remainder in a wretched and precarious state.

But here the question presents itself: When was the practice first introduced of representing St. Benedict with the Holy Cross? In answer, we may fairly quote, as some kind of origin to this practice, the very characteristic facts which we have already given from the Lives of SS. Placid and Maurus, those first founders of the traditions of the Benedictine Order. From these instances we learn how both of these saints performed their miracles by associating to the power of the Holy Cross, the merits of their master St. Benedict. But we may also find a further clue to this question in the fact related in the Life of Pope St. Leo the Ninth, who governed the Church from 1049 to 1054.

This holy Pontiff was born in the year 1002. His name was Bruno, and during his childhood he was put under the care of Berthold, Bishop of Toul. Being on a visit to some relations at the castle of Eginsheim, he was sleeping one night — it was between Saturday and Sunday — in the room which had been allotted to him. During his sleep, a frightful toad came and crept on his face. It put one of its forefeet on his ear and the other under his chin, and then, violently pressing his face, began to suck his flesh. The pressure and pain awoke Bruno. Alarmed at the danger to which he was exposed, he immediately rose from his bed, and with his hand knocked away from his ear the horrid reptile, which the moonlight enabled him to see. He immediately began to scream with fright, and several servants were soon in his room with lights; but the venomous reptile had disappeared. They searched for it in every corner of the room, but to no purpose, so that they were inclined to look upon the whole matter as a mere imagination of the boy. Be this as it may, the consequences were cruel realities, for Bruno immediately felt his face, throat and breast begin to be inflamed, and he was soon reduced to an extremely dangerous state.

For two months did his afflicted parents sit by his bedside, expecting every day to be his last. But at length, God, who destined him to become the pillar of his Church, put an end to their anxiety by restoring him to health. For eight days he had been speechless, when on a sudden, whilst perfectly awake, he saw a shining ladder which seemed to go from his bed, and then passing, through the window of his room reached up to heaven. A venerable old man, clothed in the monastic habit, and encircled with a brilliant light, descended by this ladder. He held in his right hand a cross, which was fastened to the end of a long staff. Coming close up to the sick man, he put his left hand on the ladder, and with his right placed the cross which he was carrying on Bruno's face, and afterwards on the   other parts which were inflamed. This touch caused the venom to issue through an opening which was then and there formed near the ear. The old man then departed by the same way by which he had come, leaving the sick man with the certainty of his recovery.

Bruno lost no time in calling his attendant, Adalberon, who was a cleric: he made him sit on his bed, and related to him the joyful visit which he had just received. The sadness which had overwhelmed the family was changed into an extreme joy, and in a few days the wound was healed and Bruno restored to perfect health. Ever after he loved to recount this miraculous event, and the Archdeacon Wibert, to whom we are indebted for this history, assures us that the Pontiff was convinced, that the venerable old man who had cured him by the touch of the Holy Cross, was the glorious Patriarch, St. Benedict.[1]

Such are the facts as we find them related in the Acts of St. Leo the Ninth, given by Dom Mabillon in his Sixth Benedictine Century. This history forces us to make two equally natural conjectures. First, the reason of Bruno's recognizing St. Benedict in the venerable figure which appeared to him with a cross in his hand, was because it was the custom of those times to represent the holy Legislator as bearing this sign of our redemption; and secondly, the event which we have here related, having happened to a man whose influence in the Church was so great, and who entertained such warm gratitude towards the holy Patriarch who had healed him by the cross, must have confirmed, and perhaps even originated, in Germany more particularly, where St. Leo the Ninth passed the greater part of his life, the custom of making the cross an emblem of St. Benedict, since it was the instrument whereby he worked so many wonders. The manuscript of the Metten monastery is a monument which bears witness to such being

[1] Mabillon, Acta Sanctorum Ordinis Sancte Benedicti saeculum vi.

the case, and the verses which surrounded the effigy of
the holy Patriarch were not merely the manual labor of
the anonymous writer, but a venerable formula, which was
famous even then, since the initial letters of each word
in the verses were found painted, in several parts of the
same monastery round the image of the cross, and this too
so long before, that in the year 1647 the monks were not
able to explain what the letters meant.

The affair of Nattremberg roused the devotion of the
country towards St. Benedict and his cross. In order to
secure to the faithful the protection granted by Heaven
to those who venerate the sacred cross unitedly with the
holy Patriarch of the Western Monks, certain pious persons
began to multiply and distribute, wherever they could, the
august symbols which are found on the medal. To the figure
of the cross and the effigy of St. Benedict, they added
the letters which had been explained by the Metten
manuscript. From Germany, where the medal was first struck
off, it was soon propagated into every part of Catholic
Europe, and was looked upon by the faithful as a sure
protection against the infernal spirits. St. Vincent of Paul,
who died in 1660, seems to have known this medal, for
his Sisters of Charity have always worn it attached to their
beads, and for many years it was only made, at least in
France, for them.

CHAPTER V

OF THE USE TO BE MADE OF THE
MEDAL OF ST. BENEDICT

After having described the medal of St. Benedict, and given its origin, we will now explain the use which is to be made of it and the advantages to be derived from it. We are aware that in this age of ours, when the devil is thought by many to be an imaginary rather than a real being, it will seem to be strange that a medal should be made and blessed, and used as a preservative against the power of the wicked spirit. And yet the Holy Scriptures give us abundant instructions upon the ever-busy power of the devils, as also upon the dangers to which we are exposed, both in soul and body, by the snares they set for us. The not believing in the existence of devils, or the ridiculing of the accounts which are told of their operations, is not enough to destroy their power, and, in spite of this incredulity, the air is filled with legions of these spirits of wickedness, as St. Paul teaches us.[1]

[1] Eph. ii. 2, vi. 12.

Were it not that God protected us by the ministry of the holy angels, and this generally without our being aware of it, it would be impossible for us to escape the countless snares of these enemies of all God's creatures. But if there ever was a time when it would seem to be superfluous to prove this existence of wicked spirits, it is now, when we find reappearing amongst us those dangerous and sinful practices, which were used by the pagans of old, and now again by Christians, for the purpose of eliciting an answer from spirits, though these can be no other than evil and lying ones. Surely our age is credulous enough in the existence of devils, when we find it so fashionable to be using again all those consultings of the dead, and oracles, and superstitions, which Satan employed for keeping men under his power during so many hundred years.

Now such is the power of the Holy Cross against Satan and his legions, that we may look upon it as the invincible shield which makes us invulnerable against all their darts. The brazen serpent raised up in the desert by Moses, in order to cure those who were stung by the fiery serpents, is given to us by our Savior himself as a figure of his cross.[1] The mark made on the house-doors with the blood of the Paschal Lamb by the Israelites preserved them from the terrible visit of the destroying Angel.[2] The prophet Ezechiel tells us that they were God's elect, who had *Thau* on their foreheads; and it is this same mark which St. John, in his Apocalypse, calls the sign of the Lamb.[3] It would

[1] St. John iii. 14.   [2] Exod. xii. 23.   [3] Apoc. xiv. 1.

even seem that the pagans had some idea of the power which this sacred sign was to exercise, at some future period, against the devils; for on occasion of the destruction of the temple of Serapis at Alexandria, under the Emperor Theodosius, there was found engraven upon its foundations the letters *Thau,* which is the figure of the cross, and the symbol which was venerated by the Pagans as expressive of the *future life.* The very adorers of Serapis used to say, agreeably to a tradition which they had, that when this symbol should be made known to the world, idolatry would cease.

History informs us that the pagan mysteries were sometimes rendered powerless on account of there being in the crowd a Christian who made the sign of the cross. Tertullian tells us in his "Apology," that even pagans, who had witnessed what wonders the Christians wrought by the cross, would themselves successfully employ this mysterious sign against the artifices and attacks of the wicked spirits. St. Augustine assures us that the same was done in his time: "Nor ought we," says he, "to be astonished at this; these men are, it is true, strangers who have not joined our ranks; but it is the power of our great King, which makes itself felt on these occasions."[1]

After the triumph of the Church, the great doctor, St. Athanasius, thus expressed his own convictions and confidence in reference to this important subject: "The sign of the cross," he says, "has the power of dispelling all the secret charms of magic, and of rendering harmless all the

[1] De Diversis Quaestionibus, Quaest. lxxxix.

deadly draughts it employs. Let any one but try what I say; let him make the sign of the cross in the midst of the demons, and of pretended oracles, and magical spells; let him invoke the name of Christ, and he will see for himself how the devils fly from this sign and this name, how the oracles are struck dumb, and how magic and its philters lose their power!"[1]

So that this power of the cross is, at the same time, an historical truth, and a dogma of our faith; and it is only because our faith is weak, that we so seldom have recourse to it, and so seldom experience help from it. The snares of Satan are laid for us on every side; we are surrounded by dangers both of soul and body: let us imitate the early Christians and defend ourselves by making a more frequent use of the sign of the cross. Will the happy time ever come again for our country when we shall be allowed to have the crucifix as our protection in our towns and highways and fields, and be permitted to reverence it in our public squares as well as in our own houses, and not be insulted for wearing it openly on our breast besides loving it secretly in our heart?

And now, applying these considerations to the medal which is the subject of these pages, we come to this conclusion, that it must be profitable to us to use with faith the medal of St. Benedict on occasions when we have reason to fear the snares of the enemy. Its protection will infallibly prove efficacious in every kind of temptation. Numerous and undeniable facts attest its powerful efficacy

[1] De Incarnatione Verbi, cap. xiviii.

on a thousand different occasions, in which the faithful had reason to apprehend a danger, either from the direct agency of Satan, or from the effects of certain evil practices. We may also employ it in favor of others as a means of preserving or delivering them from dangers, which we foresee are threatening them. Unforeseen accidents may happen to us on land or on sea; let us carry about us this holy medal with faith and we shall be protected. Even in the most trivial circumstances, and in those interests which regard solely man's temporal well-being, the efficacy of the holy cross and the power of St. Benedict have been felt. For example, the wicked spirits, in their hatred of man, sometimes molest the animals which God has created for our service, or infest the various articles of nourishment which the same Providence has given to us. Or again, it is not unfrequently the case that our bodily sufferings are caused or protracted by the influence of these our cruel enemies. Experience has proved that the medal of St. Benedict, made use of with a proper intention and with prayer, has frequently broken the snares of the devil, procured a visible improvement in cases of sickness, and sometimes even effected a complete cure.

CHAPTER VI

THE MIRACULOUS EFFECTS OF THE MEDAL OF
ST. BENEDICT IN THE SEVENTEENTH CENTURY

Though the medal of St. Benedict has been given to the faithful as a protection in the various necessities in which they may be at any time placed, yet as its use is only private, and almost always secret, we cannot be surprised that there has never been published an official account of the salutary effects it has produced. We are going, however, to mention some few facts which attested its powerful efficacy during the seventeenth century, the period of its first introduction into France. We take them from the pious and learned Bucelin, in his "Benedictus Redivivus" (Veldkirk, 1679, pp 267-269).

The medal, which had become well known throughout Germany after the event at Nattremberg, passed into France through the province of Franche-Comte.

In 1665, at Luxeuil in France, a young man possessed by the wicked spirit was most cruelly tormented. His parents had employed every means to free him from this state, but all had failed. In this extremity it came into their minds to have recourse to the medal of St. Benedict. They made their son drink some water into which they had dipped the medal. Scarcely had the boy raised the cup to his lips, than the devil began to torment his victim with such unusual violence, that the bystanders were struck with terror. The parents, however, were consoled by hearing the devil declare, by the mouth of their son, that he felt himself controlled by a superior power and that he would go out of the boy at the third hour of the night. So in effect it happened: the infernal spirit went out at the time mentioned, and the boy was restored to peace of mind and health of body.

The following event took place at Luxeuil about the same time. A young girl was irresistibly compelled by the wicked spirit to utter, at every turn, the most obscene words. One would have thought that the devil had taken up his abode on the lips of his victim. In order to free her from this violence of the enemy of every virtue, her friends gave her also some water to drink which had been sanctified by contact with the medal of St. Benedict. Immediately she felt herself freed from this wretched compulsion, nor did she ever after transgress in her words the rules of Christian modesty.

The same year, 1665, there was a man who had a sore on his arm, but so large and so inflamed, that no remedy seemed to have any effect on it. It was suggested that the next time the sore was dressed, there should be also tied on his arm a medal of St. Benedict. This was done, and the next day, on taking off the bandages, the sore was found to be in a healthy state, and after a few days was perfectly healed.

About the same time, another sick man was reduced to such a state that nothing seemed to give him relief, and he was despaired of. In this sad condition, he asked to be given to drink some water in which the medal of St. Benedict had been dipped, and very soon afterwards he was restored to perfect health.

In the year 1666, the castle of Maillot, not many miles from Besançon, was infested by devils. Its inmates were being continually alarmed by hearing strange noises, and numbers of their cattle were dying from unknown distempers. At length, such was the terror, that the building was abandoned. Some pious persons recommended the medal of St. Benedict being hung up here and there on the walls of the castle, and the event justified their confidence. Instantly all cause of fear disappeared, the house was perfectly quiet, and the inmates lived in it henceforth without being molested.

In 1665, a village of Lorraine was being laid waste by frequent fires. Every day some house was burnt down, and no one could discover any cause for these destructive fires. After twelve houses had been thus destroyed, the inhabitants went in despair to a neighboring monastery, and asked what they had better do under this calamity. The monks gave them several medals of St. Benedict, advising them to hang them on the walls of the houses which were still spared. The villagers followed this advice, and from that time they had no more cause to fear further ravages from fire.

In a certain part of Burgundy a distemper broke out amongst the cattle, and so virulent was it, that the cows gave blood instead of milk. They were perfectly cured on being made to drink water into which the medal of St. Benedict had been put. This happened in the same year, 1665.

The owner of a brick-kiln complained of not being able to bake the clay, no matter how intensely the kiln was heated. A medal of St. Benedict was fastened to the wall; the fire immediately regained its power, nor did the unnatural phenomenon again appear. This event happened about the same year as the last.

CHAPTER VII

During the last few years the grace of God has produced a change in the minds of the faithful of these Northern countries, by reanimating many of them with a respect for what is supernatural. This also in its turn revived confidence in the holy practices from which our ancestors received so many blessings. The medal of St. Benedict, which was on the point of becoming a secret, known only by a few pious souls, has now been brought so much into notice that thousands have recourse to it in their necessities, and their confidence has been rewarded.[1]

We proceed to give several instances of the protection granted to those who have used this holy medal, and we

---

[1] See "Vie de M. Dupont, mort à Tours en odeur de sainteté le 18 Mars 1876. Par Abbé Janvier." This work was reviewed in the "Tablet" of February 7, 1880. The subject of the memoir is said to have made great use of the medal of St. Benedict as a means of defeating the malice of Satan, and his Life is full of most interesting examples of wonderful graces obtained through its use. —ED.

begin by those which relate to the cure of bodily ailments.

In the early part of July, in the year 1843, a lady, who was taking the waters at Neris (France), was suddenly seized with a violent bleeding at the nose. The doctor is called in; he perceives the danger, but the remedies he prescribes for stopping the bleeding only seem to increase it. Things continue in this state till the evening of the third day, when, at nine o'clock, the danger visibly increases, and the doctor can no longer conceal his fears. The landlady of the hotel goes out of the room in a state of great excitement, and, as if by inspiration, she asks if any one in the house has a medal of St. Benedict. Fortunately one is found; the sick person, who was a woman of strong faith, accepts the medal, and immediately the bleeding stops. She washes her hands and face, and goes to lie down, which she had not been able to do for three days and two nights. The person who had lent the medal found, on returning home, a letter dated Rome, July 8, 1843, in which was written: "I have not yet been able to meet with the book of the 'Benedictine of Prague.'"[1] However, I send you a little book on the same subject, given me by our Benedictines of Rome." Now, in the list given in this little book of the miraculous effects of the medal of St. Benedict we read this amongst the rest: *"It is a most efficacious remedy against hemorrhage."*[2]

[1] The book here alluded to is that of Benno Löbl, Abbot of St. Margaret's of Prague, entitled, "Disquisitio sacra numismatica, de origine, quidditate, virtute, pioque usu Numismatum seu Crucularum S. Benedicti, Abbatis, Viennæ, Austriæ, apud Leopoldum Kaliwoda, 1743." We have this work, and have consulted it in drawing up this notice.

[2] "E'rimedio efficacissimo pel jetto di sangue."

About the same time, a young person, who was laid up with the typhus fever, had been obliged to sit for ten days in an arm-chair, as the reclining position of lying in bed had become unsufferable. At nine in the evening, a friend of the family, who had come to see her, spoke to her of St. Benedict's medals, and slipped one into her handkerchief. Scarce five minutes had elapsed, when the sick person got into bed, and on the morrow, after sleeping soundly during the whole night, found herself perfectly recovered from the terrible fever, which up to that time had baffled all the skill of the doctors.

In January of 1849, at T—, the Reverend Father P—, a Jesuit, called at the house of an intimate friend who lived close by, and asked him if he could recommend some cure for a toothache, which was almost driving him wild. The friend began to tell him about St. Benedict's medal. After a short explanation of it, the good Father accepts one. The very moment it touches his hand he utters a cry, like that which dentists so often hear from their patients, and then says, "My tooth is broken." He puts his finger on the place, and is surprised to find the tooth all right and the aching quite gone.

In 1858, a Benedictine of St. Paul's in Rome, having heard that a child, to which he had stood godfather, was taken dangerously ill at Juliers, in Rhenish Prussia, sent to the mother a medal of St. Benedict. Inflammation of the lungs, accompanied by spasms in the stomach, had gradually reduced the child to the last extremity. One night, the mother, seeing the child almost at the point of death, was suddenly minded to make use of the medal which she had received a few days before. Distracted with grief and trembling with anxiety, she lays the medal on her child's breast, and then throws herself on her knees at the foot of the bed in fervent prayer. That very moment the poor little sufferer quietly fell asleep, and after some hours of the most tranquil slumber, got up full of life and free from the disease, which up to that time had seemed incurable.

In the summer of the same year, 1858, the cholera was ranging at Tivoli, in Italy, and a man, who lived not far from Subiaco, was seized with the most excruciating pains. In a few hours this terrible malady had made such progress, that his friends ran in great haste to bring the priest, that he might administer the last sacraments. In the meantime the danger became so great that the sick man thought himself at the point of death, and swooned away from the violence of the pain. A few moments after he returned to himself, and felt that his sufferings were still increasing. The cramps in his stomach were more violent than ever, and in endeavoring to allay them by the pressure of his hands, he touched the medal of St. Benedict, which he always wore. This reminded him to have recourse to the holy patriarch, for whom he entertained the most lively devotion. His pains immediately disappeared; he gets up, leaves his bed, and seeing the priest, who, out of breath, with the perspiration running down his face, had just come into the house, "Father," he exclaimed, "I am cured;" and showing him the medal, he added, "See what has saved me. The good man paid a visit not long after to the

Benedictine abbey of St. Paul at Rome, taking with him the certificates of both the priest and doctor, which bore testimony to the truth of this extraordinary cure.

In February 1861, a colony of Benedictines from the same abbey of St. Paul at Rome, established itself near the town of Cleves, in Rhenish Prussia. They began in March to build an enclosure round the little garden of the new monastery. The man who acted as superintendent of repairs of the parish church, which was served by the Benedictine Fathers, offered to go and purchase for them the wood they required, for the building of the enclosure. Accordingly, he repaired to the place where they were felling trees in the Government forests. This man had given to him the medal of St. Benedict, and he carried it on his person with great devotion. After having loaded his cart with several large trunks of oak, he started back for the monastery; but just as the cart began to move, one of the trees which had not been properly fastened, came rolling down. The good man was at the back of the cart, and not being able to get out of the way in time, was knocked down and his right leg almost crushed to pieces.

He was carried home. The Prior of the monastery, on hearing of this frightful accident, said to the bystanders, "It was in the service of St. Benedict that he got wounded, and St. Benedict will cure him."

One of the religious mentioned this to the poor sufferer, who had already been thinking of having recourse to his medal, which he never ceased to wear. Placing it then on his leg, which was so fearfully crushed, he fastens it there with a bandage. In a very short time he falls fast asleep, and continued so till late the following morning, when he awakes, gets up without the slightest difficulty, and finds the wounds as perfectly healed, as though there had been no accident at all.

In 1861, at Chambery, in the convent called St. Benedict's, one of the sisters had been suffering for three months most acute pains in her legs, brought on by her having been exposed to draughts and unusually heavy work. She could not make up her mind to tell her sufferings to any one, nor had she employed any remedy. At last she resolved on making a novena in honor of St. Benedict, and during it to make use of the medal in order to obtain the protection of the holy Patriarch. During the nine days she often pressed the medal strongly upon her legs, first on one, and then on the other, at the same time invoking the aid of St. Benedict, and each time the pains were relieved. She went on, however, with the heavy work which her duties in the house required of her. The first novena not having produced any other effect than mere momentary relief, she decided on a second. This was blessed with perfect success, and entirely removed the pain. The same sister, being afterwards afflicted with sore eyes, had recourse to the same remedy, and having bathed her eyes with water into which she had dipped the medal, her sight was immediately strengthened, and in a few days became as good as ever it had been.

About the same time there lived in Savoy a little girl six years old, who had been, for several weeks, suffering the most excruciating pains. The child's nerves had become contracted, and to touch her, even with the tip of the finger, caused her to feel agonies of torture. In such a state as this, she could neither eat nor drink. Her parents had employed all the remedies which medical skill could suggest without success. The case was evidently an incurable one. Two sisters of the convent of St. Benedict, which we have just mentioned, went to visit the little girl (for she belonged to the school which they managed), and to offer some consolation to the mother. On reaching home they bethought themselves of the medal of St. Benedict. They immediately sent one, with word that it should be put round the child's neck, and that she should be persuaded to swallow something into which the medal should have been previously dipped. The mother of the little sufferer faithfully complied with the pious prescription. An immediate change was visible, and after a few days the child got up perfectly cured.

In the same country, but in the preceding year, two women were cured — one of the miliary fever after confinement, and the other of a dangerous attack of dropsy on the chest — and both of them by drinking something into which the medal of St. Benedict had been put.

In the district of Westmoreland, Pennsylvania, during the month of August 1861, Mrs. X, a Catholic, perceived that one of her daughters was taken with a violent attack of diphtheria. It began about evening, and kept getting worse every hour. It was the more distressing owing to the difficulty of finding a doctor in that part of the country. The nearest was almost twelve miles away. The mother had great faith in the protection of St. Benedict, and had one of his medals in her possession. She resolved on putting this medal into a tumbler of water, and making her child drink it.   She did so. The child drank the water thus sanctified by the contact of the medal, and next morning was out of all danger.

In the early part of the year 1863, at Montigny-le-Roy, there was a woman who had been suffering for a long time the most severe attacks of earache. Clots of blood and bad matter would occasionally come forth from the ear, showing the diseased state of the organ. At length deafness came on, and the poor woman was unfit for any work. Having had a medal of St. Benedict given to her, she put it to her ear, and said a Pater and Ave in honor of the holy Patriarch. The moment after, she was completely cured, and could hear as well as ever she had done in her life.

The same year, at Andabres (Dep. de Herault), Miss R. G. was for two years threatened with a cancer on the forehead. A painful gland had formed on it, and had resisted all the remedies which medical men had employed to cure it. One evening, before retiring to rest, this young lady thought of placing on her forehead, during the night, a medal of St. Benedict, at the same time earnestly recommending herself to the holy Patriarch's protection. She slept most soundly that night, and next morning, after taking off the medal, found to her surprise, that the gland had entirely disappeared.

At Limoges, in the year 1864, in the house of the Sisters of St. Joseph, a postulant came to show one of her superiors her arm, in which some foreign body had entered. She was suffering most acute pains, and this led to the conjecture, that a needle had entered the flesh; and on feeling the arm it seemed evident, that certainly something of that nature must have entered. A surgeon was sent for, in the hope that by lancing the arm the poor creature might be somewhat relieved. All at once, before the doctor arrived even, the idea struck the assistant sister of having recourse to the medal of St. Benedict. She placed it straightway on the wounded arm. After having recited together five Our Fathers and five Hail Marys, with the invocation to St. Benedict, the postulant said, "Suppose I try to draw out the needle?" "Try," answered the assistant sister. Their efforts were not of the slightest avail, and tended only to increase the pain. The assistant then said to the sister, "Press with the medal on one side." The sister obeyed. Scarcely had she pressed it upon one side of the arm, than the needle appeared on the other, and they were able to draw it out easily, and that without causing pain. When the surgeon arrived, his services were not required.

At Montauban, in the year 1865, an invalid lady, unable to move, was confined to her bed for two years and a half, and everything seemed to forbode that she would remain thus helpless the rest of her life. One day after the priest had brought her Holy Communion, a Sister of Charity, who had just come on her accustomed visit, with some difficulty managed to place the medal of St. Benedict between her fingers, and succeeded with great exertion in bringing the hand of the sick lady to rest upon her breast, hoping the touch of this sacred object would produce some good result.

Immediately the invalid felt a thrill throughout her whole being, a copious perspiration broke out, and these words escaped her lips, "I am cured!" At once life returned to her limbs; she attempted to rise, and ridding herself of the flannels in which she had been swathed for so long a time, put on once more the clothes which she had been in the habit of wearing before her sickness. As early as the following day, she betook herself to the church to give thanks to God for her sudden cure.

Madame A. S., a lady of the diocese of Le Mans, in the year 1868, suffered intense pains in the head from neuralgia, which was caused by a decayed tooth. All ordinary remedies had been tried, and none had had any effect. The patient had recourse to the medal of St. Benedict, and pressing it close to her cheek, held it there; but it gave her no relief. After the lapse of about half an hour, all the time holding the medal to her cheek, she received a visit from a neighboring friend, who had just been acquainted with the news of her illness, and the sick woman gave him an account, in a disconnected manner, of the violence of her sufferings. Her visitor, seized with compassion, suggested that perhaps a little brandy kept in her mouth for a short time, would at least deaden the pain a little. As there was no brandy in the house, he sent to his own home a person who was present, to get some, charging him to return with it quickly.

Scarcely had the messenger closed the door behind him, than the pain stopped suddenly, never more to return. St. Benedict, whose medal had been used, only after medical aid had proved useless, would not allow material means to succeed, after use had been made of the glorious emblem of his power, and the cure of the poor sufferer was instantaneous.

CHAPTER VIII

ON THE SPIRITUAL FAVORS OBTAINED
BY THE USE OF THE MEDAL

The greater number of favors obtained during our own times, by means of St. Benedict's medal, have reference to the instantaneous conversion of sinners, who had been callous to all that had previously been tried, in order to bring them to God. We will mention a few of these instances.

In a provincial town of France, there was living a gentleman in very comfortable circumstances, who had once held a Government appointment. His sister, an exceedingly pious widowed lady nursed him with the most affectionate care during his frequent attacks of illness, but was, above all, most anxious to induce her dear brother to think upon doing something for his salvation. Hitherto, all her efforts had been fruitless. No matter how gentle or indirect her attempts, they were all met with this cold answer, "Do not talk to me about seeing a priest; I cannot bear to hear the subject mentioned." The sister went, at last, to a friend, and told him in confidence of her trouble, and he said to her, "Pay no attention to your brother's answer; persevere in your entreaties. If by your silence you suffer him to fall into hell, he would surely not excuse you." In this way several years elapsed.

In the December of 1846, after a short illness, there were evidences of gangrene; the doctors not only pronounced such to be the case, but moreover, that an operation would be useless, and finally, that the sick man could not live two days longer. The friend who had advised the sister not to be deterred by the words of her brother, one day came to see her. She was overwhelmed with grief, but declared, that not even now, had she the courage to put the question to him. "Well, then," says the friend, "take these two medals of St. Benedict; keep one for yourself that the devil may not hinder you from doing your duty, and put the other under your brother's pillow." She took his advice, and five minutes had scarcely passed, when the following conversation took place between the brother and sister:-"Dear sister!" said the sick man. "Well, brother, what is it?" "My dear sister, do you not think it would be right to send for the priest?" The Priest was accordingly sent for, and soon arrived: the sick man received him with joy, and all the rites of the Church were administered. Two days after he died in the most edifying dispositions.

In 1854, in an hospital of incurables, there was a woman advanced in years, who was almost entirely paralysed, and quite bedridden. With no more religion

about her than that of an impious lunatic, she would utter
at times such disgusting language and such horrid
blasphemies, that many persons looked upon her as one
possessed by the devil. There were reasons for suspect-
ing that she kept near her certain articles, which prompted
her to all this wickedness. It happened that on a day,
when the ward had to undergo a thorough cleaning, she
was obliged to be taken from her bed, and put for the
time in a room near at hand. She screamed, or rather
howled, with rage, but she was obliged to yield. The nuns
of the hospital found under the mattress a bag filled with
objects of a most suspicious character. They took it away,
and put in its place a medal of St. Benedict. In an hour
or so the poor woman was carried back to her bed, without
of course being told of what had been done. Scarcely,
however, did she come near the bed than she began to
abuse the sisters for having taken away her treasure, of
which no doubt the devil took care to tell her.   In spite
of all this, she was laid on the bed, when suddenly her
screaming ceased, and she became as quiet as a lamb.
The hideous look she ordinarily put on was changed into
one of joy. The poor creature then asked for a priest.
A few days after the infirmary was arranged as a chapel,
prettily lit up, and flowers placed here and there, to
receive our Lord, who was coming to comfort and cure
this soul, now set free, like a captive bird, from the snares
of hell.

In 1859, a poor woman was telling her troubles to a
person, who knew something of the efficacy, with which

our Lord has enriched the medal of St. Benedict. Her husband, though a clever workman, was a great drunkard. All they earned was regularly spent at the end of the week, and, of course, there was nothing in the house but wretchedness. The person to whom she spoke gave her one of the medals, advising her to touch with it the bottle of wine, which she put before her husband at meals, though she herself was obliged to be satisfied with water. When he had tested the wine, he exclaimed, "What wretched stuff! give me some water, for it is better than such wine as this. I will make up for it after." When he had finished his dinner, he made his wife give him some money, and went to his old place, the neighboring public house, from which he was always accustomed to come back home, late at night, intoxicated. In about a quarter of an hour he came home, telling his wife that he was sure this was a plot against him, for the wine at the tavern was worse than their own. It was a happy night for both. Next day, and the next few days, water was the only beverage the poor man could bear to touch. When this much was gained, his wife, who was an excellent Christian, had not much difficulty in persuading him to fulfill henceforward his religious duties.

In the same year, 1859, at T——, there was a woman, eighty years old, who had declared that she was determined to die without going to confession; it was upwards of sixty years since she had been to the Sacraments. The priest, who was asked by a friend to visit her, was prepared for a refusal. A medal was put into the priest's hand, and the person who gave it to him said, "Go, and fear not." On his entering her room, the old lady turned her face towards the wall, saying aloud that she intended going to sleep. "Do so," replied the priest, "but take this medal, I beg of you, and meanwhile I will say a little prayer." He knelt down by the bedside, and before he had time to finish the Memorare, the old lady turned towards him, told her relatives to leave the room, and began her confession.

On the 14th of March, 1859, a pious layman happened to meet in the street a priest, who was much distressed about a young man of seventeen who had come home from Paris so ill, that the doctor was of opinion that he could not live many days. The priest had been three times to the house, but the family would not receive him. The layman on hearing this, spoke to him about the wonderful efficacy of St. Benedict's medal, gave him one, and encouraged him to make another trial. The priest went, and at first met with the same reception. He then brought forth the medal, which he said he wished to give to the young man. "Oh, if that is all," said the person, who was speaking to him, "you may come in." Finally, he got into the room of the young man, who no sooner saw him than he hid his face in the bedclothes. "My dear friend," said the priest, "accept this little present from me." Immediately he uncovered his face, and began his confession with the most admirable sentiments of contrition.

In 1860, an old man was received into one of the Paris

hospitals, and falling seriously ill there, it was evident that he had but a very short time to live. He was a Protestant. The sisters, who had the care of the hospital, seeing that there was no chance of his recovery, lost no time in making every possible effort to secure to him the life of the soul. For this end they had made novena after novena; private and general communions had been offered up, and they had got a great many masses said. It seemed, however, to be all of no avail. It happened one Sunday, that a friend   having come to the hospital to visit the sick, and being informed of the poor Protestant who was so near death, advised them to give the sick man a medal of St. Benedict, and in case he should refuse it, to put it under his pillow. The advice was instantly followed, and the medal was put round the neck of the dying man. The next time the same person came to the hospital, he had the consolation of hearing, that the very Sunday he advised them to use the medal, the Protestant had asked at twelve o'clock at night to be received into the Church. They offered to send for either of the two nearest parish priests, but he refused, saying that he would prefer the chaplain of the house, whom he happened to know. This latter, not having the faculties necessary for receiving the sick man's abjuration or for absolving him from heresy, leave was obliged to be sent for to the Archbishop, so that in spite of all the diligence that was used, it was not possible to administer the Sacraments to the sick man before nine o'clock the next morning. The old man received all the rites of the Church with great devotion, and died tranquilly in the evening of the same day.

An English Puseyite minister, a young man full of information, happened to be at T— in 1861. He was fond of controversy, and had therefore sought an introduction to three parsons who had become zealous converts, and lived out in the country not far from the town. For nine days had the amicable discussion been going on with no result. The tenth day, May 14th, was fixed by Divine Providence for the close of these disputes, which were destined to prepare the way for an extraordinary conversion. The Puseyite minister was going back to the town, and one of his three friends being obliged to take a party of children to see the circus, which was at that time being exhibited in a field adjoining the market-place, invited him to go there with them. He did so. They reached the circus and took their tickets. Whilst the children were enjoying the amusements, our two controversialists resumed their discussion, and as their neighbors could not understand them, they were under no restraints. The entertainment was about half over, when the Puseyite interrupted the dispute, saying, "I have had quite enough; let us have no more; you can never convince me." Thus abruptly silenced, his Catholic friend was going to give all up, when he suddenly bethought himself of the wonderful things he had heard regarding the medal of St. Benedict, and taking off the one he wore, he begged his friend to accept it. The Puseyite holds out his hand and takes the medal. For several minutes there was silence on both sides. Meanwhile the Catholic was praying.

Suddenly the Puseyite broke the silence with these words: "My dear friend, I have done wrong by holding all these long disputes. The light now beams upon me, and I wish without delay to be received into the Church." Accordingly, he made his profession of faith five days after, and the Church numbered one more in the fold of Christ.

In the town of Noyon, in France, there was a pious workwoman, who was in great trouble on account of her mother being out of her mind, and having fits from time to time, during which she was perfectly furious. People who brought work to the daughter were afraid of the poor mad mother, who would sometimes seize anything she could get hold of in the room, and throw it out of the window. There was every reason for fearing that some day or other she would destroy herself. This state of things went on for several years. But there was nothing which so afflicted the daughter as the impossibility of her mother ever getting to confession, which was the more distressing as this state of madness had seized the poor creature so suddenly, that she had not had the opportunity of settling the affairs of her conscience. In the year 1861, a pious Christian happened to give her a medal of St. Benedict, which she contrived to put round her mother's neck. In that same instant all her madness ceased — she took the medal and kissed it unceasingly. Soon after, she made her confession in the most edifying manner. Since then, she has continued to be as gentle and quiet as a lamb, and though the infirmities of old age now oblige her to keep her bed, she never gives way to anything like impatience, and there seems to be every likelihood of her dying a happy death.[1]

[1] See Life of St. Benedict, chap. xxxviii.

CHAPTER IX

PROTECTION AGAINST THE SNARES OF THE DEVIL[1]

There is one special influence which the medal of the holy Patriarch St. Benedict possesses, and which may be called the principal object for which God has given this gift to the faithful — the power it possesses to frustrate the devil's stratagems. We here mention a few facts which will do more than merely interest our readers; they will suggest to them what they themselves may do, should they ever find themselves in circumstances which now-a-days are anything but impossible.

In 1839, a celebrated magnetizer, who had performed several wonderful things in different towns in France, stopped at T—, where he advertised that he was going to give public performances. He took about with him to all these different places a young girl on whom he exercised his mesmerism, and he drew crowded audiences by the extraordinary effects be produced on this poor victim. In

[1] See Life of St. Benedict, chap. xvi., xxx.

the town of which we are now speaking, he attracted an immense crowd by his advertisement. The lecture was to be given in a very large room, which anciently had been a church, but had been turned to profane uses long before this. The hour came; but nothing that the magnetizer did, had the slightest effect, and the girl remained unmoved by all his passes. The audience was dismissed, and the money returned to those who grumbled at being disappointed. A few hours after, placards were plastered up all over the town, announcing a second meeting, at such an hour, in the Town Hall. But this time also, the lecturer could do nothing, and after all his trouble and expense, he stole away from the town. Next day came the papers with their scientific explanations of the failure. One would have it that the room had been too hot, another that the gas was too much turned on, and the rest. Of course, none of them assigned the true cause. A nun who had happened to hear of the proposed lecture, and knowing that the Church is opposed to the practice of mesmerism, resolved on thwarting the operations of the lecturer, so far as they had any connection with the devil. All she did was to hang out of her cell window a medal of St. Benedict, and beg the intervention of the holy Patriarch. The result was what we have related, and *the prince of the power of this air,*[1] as the Apostle calls Satan, was vanquished.

In the year 1840, the town council of S— proposed to widen one of the streets, though it was already quite wide

[1] Eph. ii. 2.

enough for the traffic. The measure was carried, and it was resolved that they should pull down a large portion of a church dedicated to our Blessed Lady, and much frequented by pilgrims. In order to carry out this plan, they began to build a partition wall the whole length of the church. Our Lady's altar was within the part to be taken down, and therefore was to be destroyed by this whim of the street commissioners. The wall had risen twenty feet, and one may imagine the mess and confusion in the church caused by the masons. A gentleman who was passing through the town, was grieved to see such a sad profanation, and going up to the statue of our Lady, which had been brought from its own place into the portion of the church which was to be spared, he put a medal of St. Benedict on the pedestal. A few days after, the town surveyor, who had been mainly instrumental in this measure, died suddenly. His successor, when coming to inspect the works, soon perceived how totally unnecessary such a change was, even were it not a desecration, and stopped the works. The next day, he went before the town council and submitted to its consideration so satisfactory a report upon the matter, that the first decision was revoked. The wall, which had almost reached as high as the ceiling, was taken down, and the people saw their dear old church given back to them.

In one of our French towns, a certain gentleman of high position, placed over some most important works, had in his employ a man whom the enemy of all good made use of as a tool, to lessen the influence of his master. All hopes of his amendment had been abandoned, and the evil increased day by day, when some one in the establishment put a medal of St. Benedict over the framework of the room-door of this man who had proved so mischievous in his position of trust. From that time forward to remain in the room became next to impossible for him. On the 20th of March 18—, at twelve o'clock, the hour at which the first vespers of St. Benedict were ending, on account of its being Lent,[1] he threw up his employment, and on the following day, which was the feast of St. Benedict, he quitted the establishment.

Not far from the city of Rennes, there was a cafe and billiard-room kept by a good Catholic family. For some years they had noticed strange symptoms of the place being infested with demons. When there was no one at the billiard-table, noises and voices were sometimes heard as though there were a large party playing; pieces of furniture were changed from place to place in the house without any one of the family touching them; doors opened and shut apparently of themselves, and a strange noise was heard in the bedrooms. One Christmas night, the servant had gone up to the attic to get herself ready for midnight Mass, when she found all that part of the house filled with a thick smoke, in the midst of which there was a something, which she could not lay hold of, moving to and fro. She screamed,

---

[1] The ancient discipline of the Church was not to break the fast before Vespers (sunset). Therefore in Lent, from the first Sunday, to observe this very ancient tradition, Vespers are anticipated and recited before the time when the principal meal is allowed to be taken. —Ed.

hurried out of the place, and fainted. But these strange
appearances were frequently happening, and of course kept
the inmates of the house in a state of continual alarm. They
had got many masses said for the dead, and had had the
house blessed with the formula prescribed by the Church
for these occasions, but up to that time all had proved
ineffectual. Nothing, therefore, remained for the inmates of
the house but to abandon it, though it was quite new, and
they had hoped to find it a convenient and comfortable home.
A pious woman spoke to them about St. Benedict's medal,
and persuaded them to make use of it. They began by putting
it over every door in the house, and immediately all was
quiet. But they had not thought of placing the sign of
salvation in the doorway leading to the cellar, and all the
fury of the evil spirits seemed to concentrate there, so great
was the noise and disorder which began to be heard from
that quarter. The medal was put there also, and the influence
of Satan seemed at last to have entirely quitted the house;
not, however, without seeking his revenge by there and then
taking possession of the person who related all this to the
writer. Cruel indeed were the sufferings which the devil
caused his victim to endure both in body and soul. This
person, however, obtained, after some time, deliverance from
this terrible trial by following the counsels of an enlightened
director, who recommended the poor sufferer not to be afraid
of the devil, and to pronounce frequently the holy names
of Jesus, Mary, and Joseph.

In the year 1863, a community of nuns, who kept a
boarding-school at A—, noticed that first the glass-lamps

in the study place, and then those in the refectory of the boarding-school, were by turns broken. The drinking glasses of the lay-sisters, in like manner, were found broken in the refectory drawers. No system of supervision was able to bring to light the cause of the mischief, which was of daily occurrence. This state of affairs lasted for several weeks, when the idea came to the mind of one of the sisters of having recourse to the medal of St. Benedict. The nuns put this medal in the lamps and in the drawers, and forthwith the accidents ceased. But what was more astonishing still, was, that the lamps which lighted the galleries and the other rooms of the house were now attacked in their turn, and the breakages began again worse than ever. They only ceased, after the sisters had taken the resolution of employing the same means, which had been so successful in the study room and refectory of the establishment. Then at last were they freed from all further annoyances.

CHAPTER X

THE MEDAL A PRESERVATION IN DANGER

Amongst the effects of St. Benedict's medal, when it is employed with a lively and simple faith, has always been ranked that of protecting us in danger. We here offer to the reader a few recent facts, which will show that the power granted to this medal by Almighty God is far from being exhausted.

In June 1847, four Christian brothers and two other travelers were going by coach from Orleans to Lyons. They were inside passengers, and one of the gentlemen began to speak to the rest about St. Benedict's medal, and gave one to each of the party. He was busy explaining to them the meaning of the letters, when on a sudden the horses took fright at something, set off at full gallop, and the driver soon lost all command over them. The road was being mended, and one half of the pavement had been taken up. The stones with which the road was going to be repaved had been piled up in such a manner as to serve as a barrier to keep conveyances from going on the part which was unpaved. The horses dashed across this heap of stones, dragging the coach after them. Though one side was fearfully higher than the other, it was not upset. For two or three minutes it ploughed through the soft ground on the other side of the road, then in the twinkling of an eye was dragged back again, all safe on to the good part; and as the traces were broken by the violence of the shock, it immediately stopped, much to the relief of the passengers. This happened near a village called Chateau-Neuf (Loiret), which is about six miles from the town of Saint-Benoit-sur-Loire. The people of the village, who had witnessed the narrow escape of the conveyance, cried out, "It is a miracle! What else could have saved it?"

A few years before this, in June 1843, a diligence was going up the very steep hill near Ecommoy, a village on the highroad between Le Mans and Tours. The horses were not able to proceed, and, suddenly stopping, were dragged back down the hill at a fearful speed. There were three passengers in the front compartment of the diligence. Opening the door, two of them jumped out on the road, but the third kept his seat, and took into his hands his medal of St. Benedict. That very instant the diligence stopped, and the horses, which had been dragged sideways, quietly returned to the middle of the road.

It was a summer's day in the year 1858, about five o'clock in the afternoon, when a wagon heavily laden with goods was passing along the street called Rue Royale, Saint Honore, in Paris. It had got opposite No. 4 or 6, when it stopped. It was in the middle of the street. The horses became restive, and a crowd soon collected. One of the traces broke and the front horse turned completely round. He seemed wild with fright. He raised himself upon his hind legs, and throwing up his other two as high as he could, came down with his whole weight upon another of the horses, which he began biting most savagely, and this done, he recommenced his prancing and kicking. The wagoner was most vigorous in his attempts to subdue the poor animal, pulling the reins and dealing the hardest blows he could, on the horse's head with the butt-end of the whip; but all this seemed only to irritate him the more and make things worse. The policeman who was on the spot assisted the driver in his attempts, and the spectators were busy, as usual on such occasions, vociferating their advice, and yet all to no effect. In the crowd there was a good Christian who had learned by experience how powerful is the intercession of St. Benedict. Seeing the danger, he took the medal in his hand, at the same time addressing a short ejaculation to the holy Patriarch. Scarcely had his lips pronounced the prayer, when the horse, which was still wild with rage, became suddenly quiet, allowing himself to be patted and then led to his place.

One beautiful morning of the same summer, and in the same city, two soldiers in half-uniform had been giving some exercise to the horses of which they had the management. They were returning to barracks and had arrived opposite the mayor's courthouse of district No. 1, when the following scene took place, and attracted the attention of the idle and curious who were passing along the street called Rue Anjou,

Saint Honore.   One of the horses suddenly stopped, and
turning sideways, nothing that his rider did could induce
the animal to move.[1] In front of the courthouse was an open
space. It was facing this that the horse stood just as though
he were riveted to the earth. Every now and then he shook
his whole body. One of the passersby was a person who
had great faith in the medal of St. Benedict: he had not quite
come up to the spot, but as well as he could judge at the
distance, he could not help thinking that the enemy of
mankind might very possibly have something to do with
all this. Afraid of an accident happening, he recited to himself
the words of which the initials are engraven on the medal:
Vade retro, Satana, etc. No sooner had he finished the
formula, than the horse began to prance and rear, and then
became immovable as before.

The individual of whom we just spoke, and who was
now very near to the courthouse, perceiving that the rider
was still in the same difficulty, took his medal into his
hand, and said this little prayer: "Glorious St. Benedict,
beseech our Lord that He, by thy intercession, may make
these horses docile to the command of their riders, and deliver
them from danger." The stubborn animal at once proceeded
quietly onwards, and cantered up to the other, which had
been waiting. The unknown liberator asked a woman who
was standing on the pavement at the corner of the street
Suresnes, if the horses had been standing there a long time.
She told him they had been there for a quarter of an hour.

---

[1] See Life of St. Benedict, chap. ix.

During the winter of 1858-59, the same person was in Paris, and was just turning into the street Miromesnil. His attention was attracted by seeing a crowd standing on the footpath opposite this street; and the stoppage, he found, was caused by a horse which would not stir one inch farther, in spite of all the beating and spurring of the groom who was riding him. Anxious to see what was the matter, he stopped, and saw that the animal obstinately refused to proceed. The groom at length was obliged to rest, and called for a glass of something to drink to revive his courage and strength. Thinking that Satan might have something to do with such strange perversity, the person we allude to, resolved on having recourse to his medal of St. Benedict. Scarcely had he finished the words which are marked on the medal, than the horse set off at a gallop along the Avenue Marigny. In spite of this, he still feared the snares of the invisible enemy, so whilst proceeding on his way he kept his eyes on the horse and rider. His fears were soon realised, for the horse had not gone half-way up the avenue, when he suddenly stopped again and turned round as before. The good man then took his medal into his hand, and said this short prayer: "O glorious St. Benedict, ask of our Lord that He may, by thy intercession, render this His creature obedient to man and harmless." The horse instantly became tractable, and the groom turning him to the right into the Champs Elysees, they soon were out of sight.

On Sunday, the 28th of November 1858, Henry S— a boy of fourteen, who was apprenticed to M. P—, a jeweler in Paris, happened to meet in the street a person whom he knew to be a friend who took an interest in his family. After a cordial greeting and a few words of conversation, the young man received from the friend a medal of St. Benedict, as a protection against the dangers to which we are all so much exposed. On the following Thursday, which was the 2nd of December, our young apprentice was sliding down the banisters of the staircase, when, seeing that some one was coming up, and afraid of coming against him, he leaned forward, lost his balance, and fell down nearly two stories. In his fall, he came with his side against the banister of the lower story, and the violence of the shock sent him back on to the last step of the landing, where he found himself sitting, with no other injury than being stunned by the fall. He immediately returned to the workshop and resumed his employment. His master, however, fearing that such an accident might produce some fatal result, in spite of there being nothing just then which could give the slightest ground of alarm, sent him home for a few days' perfect rest. Nothing, however, like an indisposition came on, and the young man could not help attributing his extraordinary escape to the power of St. Benedict's medal, which had so very opportunely been given him to wear.

At Tours, in 1859, a young gentleman was taking a lesson of exercises at a public gymnasium of the town. He was going through one of the feats, which consisted in pulling himself up to a horizontal beam, on which he was then to hang, holding on by his hands and feet. He had scarcely accomplished this than the beam gave way, and he fell fifteen feet flat upon his back on the ground with the beam upon him. The master of the gymnasium, who was present, uttered a cry of alarm; but the young man jumped up, and taking his medal of St. Benedict showed it to him, saying, "I am all right! I assure you I am not hurt! See what has saved me."

In the February of 1859, a nurse happened to be walking with a little child in the gardens of the Tuileries. It was about three o'clock in the afternoon, and the Emperor was passing. The nurse could not resist her curiosity, so she set off running by the side of the Emperor's carriage, was soon lost in the thick of the crowd, and forgot all about her little charge whom she left behind. The little fellow, seeing himself thus left alone, began to make his way home, which was in the street called Rue Saint Florentin, No. 4. There was a perfect stream of carriages passing just at this exciting moment along the Rue de Rivoli, but the brave little fellow was not afraid. He boldly crossed the street and reached home. His parents were alarmed at seeing him come home by himself; they asked him how he had lost his nurse, and when his sister, who was a year or so older than himself, was exclaiming and asking how in the world he had got home without being run over, "I had round my neck the medal of St. Benedict," said the child very coolly; "and just as I was going to cross the street, the carriages made such a noise! But they let me run across."

In 1859, a community of nuns, whose special object was the education of young ladies, had just finished building a large dormitory for their boarders. It was now ready for use, and both parents and children were delighted with the excellent accommodation which the new building afforded, for besides the dormitory there were also several parlors on the ground-floor. But not many weeks elapsed, before much alarm was caused by crackings being heard all over the building. At first they were thought to be the creaking which is sometimes heard in rooms newly boarded; but they became so loud and threatening, that the parents began to talk of taking their children from the school. In vain did the architect assure them that the building was perfectly safe; the nuns were obliged to pacify them by removing all the children from the new dormitory and promising every possible precaution against accident. They would have begun at once to build another dormitory, but they had spent all their available funds over the one which now proved such a disappointment. A friend of the convent, to whom two of the nuns happened to mention their trouble, advised their having recourse to St. Benedict. He recommended them to put a medal of the holy Patriarch on each story of the new building, and four down into the foundations, one on each side, reciting meanwhile five times *Gloria Patri* in honor of the Passion, three times *Ave Maria* in honor of Our Lady, and lastly, three times *Glorià Patri* in honor of St. Benedict. His advice was followed; nothing more was heard of the noises which had caused so much alarm, and the community returned fervent thanks to God, to Our Lady, and to St. Benedict, for the protection thus visibly granted to them.

In July 1859, at Paris, a gentleman was passing on horseback up the Avenue Gabrielle. He happened to come

up to that part of the Avenue which is at the back of the
Elysee Garden, just as one of the gardeners was watering
the beds with one of the large tubes. A cart loaded with
wood had been stopped in this very place, in consequence
of an accident which had happened to a carriage. The gush
of the watering machine frightened the gentleman's horse,
which suddenly turning round, galloped back some distance.
The rider encouraged the animal to return, and shouted out
to the gardener to stop watering for a moment whilst he
passed. No attention was paid to this request, and the horse
again shied, and again galloped back. Once more the rider
urged him by spur and whip to the dreaded spot, and at
a furious speed he at last passed it, but in doing so, came
with such a shock against the wheel of the cart, that the
girth of the saddle was torn and the stirrups got twisted.
The gentleman had foreseen the danger, and had pulled
his foot out of the stirrup, but in doing so he threw himself
so much on the other side as completely to lose his balance,
and was thrown over the head of his horse, which passed
over him without trampling on him. The poor animal had
taken fright at the shower of water which came spurting
out in every direction, and though the rider had done his
best to pull him clear from the cart, which stood, as we
have said, upon the road, yet he dashed against it with
all his weight. The gentleman had on his person the medal
of St. Benedict, and felt nothing whatever from the fall
but a little stiffness in his limbs. The horse was badly cut
by the cart-wheel on his side and hind leg, and for twelve
days was unfit for use. The saddle was taken to a saddler

in the street Suresnes, and several persons who had witnessed the accident expressed to the rider their surprise at
his having escaped without a single scar.

A medal of St. Benedict had been given to a poor woman
who had just lost her husband, and was living by herself
in a lonely cottage some distance from Rennes (in France).
She was extremely nervous at having to live thus alone
and as a protection against danger she accepted the medal
from a good Christian who lived in the town. In the year
1862, an unhappy wretch, who had just come out of prison,
was prowling all about the neighborhood. He at last hit
on a plan for getting into some of the houses round about:
he would set the widow's cottage on fire — the people
of the neighborhood would leave their houses and run to
the spot, and whilst they were out, he might go in and
do his work. An opportunity soon presented itself. The
poor widow was spending an hour or two with a neighbor.
Suddenly she felt unusually anxious, and declared that she
must go home. She is no sooner there than she sees a
cloud of smoke coming from the little stable adjoining her
cottage, and a man running across the field as though he
were trying to make his escape. Without giving herself time
for reflection, she set off running after the man, and was
not long in discovering him to be the very individual who,
not long before, had come to her door begging for something to drink. Whilst pursuing him she screamed for help,
and a farmer hearing her, rushed out of his house with
his servants, and recognised in the fugitive the man who
had attacked him only a few nights before. They were not

long before they caught him. He was handed over to the police, and finally sentenced to fourteen years' penal servitude. When in court, he confessed publicly that he had done his utmost to set fire to the widow's cottage, but not being able to succeed, he threw a lighted faggot into the stable, and then went his way. His attempt to burn down the house did not do the slightest injury either to the stable or to the house.

During the month of April 1864, M. D—, of the city of Tours, narrated to us the following incident: He was a visitor at the watering-place of Bourbon-Sancy, during the summer months of one of the preceding years, when a thunderbolt happened to strike one of the houses there and reduced it to ashes. One room only, occupied by two poor girls, escaped destruction. No one could explain so unaccountable an escape, so that all the town flocked to gaze at this marvel. M. D— also betook himself to the spot in company with some of the bathers. After having closely examined the arrangement of the various portions of the building, and listened to the story of the inhabitants, he had no hesitation in believing that there had taken place some supernatural intervention. He even felt within himself that St. Benedict had not been a stranger to the event, and taking from his pocket a medal of the holy Patriarch, he offered it to these good young girls. But hardly had they caught sight of the little present he was offering them, when they exclaimed, "But we already have that medal. Yesterday our brother, having been to water some horses, met a person who had some of those medals, and knowing that it would give us great pleasure, he asked for one, which he brought home to us *some minutes before the storm.*"

CHAPTER XI

APPROBATION OF ST. BENEDICT'S
MEDAL BY THE HOLY SEE

The above facts, and many others of the same kind which we pass over in silence, naturally suggest the question as to whether the authority of the Church has spoken on the subject of a devotion, the results of which will probably excite as much astonishment in the minds of some, as they will give confidence and comfort to others. Fortunately the Holy See has long since examined the subject upon which we are now writing, and has given to the medal of St. Benedict the wished-for sanction, which is an authority and an argument superior even to those which are given by the wonderful instances of its efficacy, which are every day being related as having taken place in almost every country. The medal had been attacked as savoring of superstition by the too famous J. B. Thiers, author of the "Treatise on Superstitions"[1] — a work, by the way, which is on the Index.

[1] J. B. Thiers was curate of Vibraye, in the diocese Le Mans, France. Obit A.D. 1703.

This unreasonable critic defended his opinion regarding the medal by this strange argument: that the initial letters which are upon it are difficult to be understood, and are therefore to be suspected of some superstitious purpose.

It was reserved to the learned Pope Benedict XIV to encourage the faithful in their confidence in this holy medal, and to confute the scruples which the rationalism of that period endeavored to raise regarding it. At the request of Dom. Benno Löbl, Abbot of St. Margaret's monastery in Prague, this Pontiff, after a careful examination, and a decree of the Congregation of Indulgences, approved by his Brief of March I2, 1742, the medal with the cross, the effigy of St. Benedict, and the letters which are upon it. He authorised the form of blessing which is to be used over this medal, and granted a great number of indulgences to all who carry it about with them. We here give the text of this important Brief, for it is but too little known:

BENEDICT XIV, POPE

BENEDICTUS P. P. XIV

Unto the perpetual memory thereof, and for the increasing of the devotion of the faithful of Jesus Christ. Watchful, with fatherly love, over the heavenly treasures of the Church, and desirous of enriching with the grant of

Ad perpetuam rei memoriam, et ad augendam Christi fidelium devotionem.

Cœlestibus ecclesiæ thesauris paterna charitate intenti, sacra interdum numismata, seu cruces, vel cruc-

indulgences the sacred medals, known under the name of crosses or little crosses of St. Benedict, we have gladly accorded to certain persons holding certain dignities, the special power to bless the said medals with rich indulgences, and to distribute them amongst the faithful; and to the end that this grant may produce its full effect, and abide uninterrupted in all future time, the more especially as such has been asked of us, we willingly add hereunto the weight of apostolic confirmation, and the influence of our endeavors and solicitude, according as it has seemed to us before God, to be good and needful, having maturely considered the circumstances of persons, places, and times.

Our beloved son Benno Löbl, professed monk of the

ulas Sancti Benedicti nuncupatas, indulgentiarum muneribus condecorare voluimus; et personis, præsertim speciali dignitate fulgentibus, facultatem illas cum thesauro indulgentiarum hujusmodi privative benedicendi et distribuendi libenter impartiti fuimus; et ut illa perpetuis futuris temporibus suum plenarium sortiatur effectum, firmiusque persistat; potissimum quum a nobis petitur, apostolicæ confirmationis robur libenter adjicimus, opemque et operas nostras impendimus efficaces, prout personarum, locorum, et temporum qualitatibus matura consideratione pensatis, in Domino conspicimus Salubriter expedire.

Exponi nobis nuper sane fecit dilectus filius Benno Lobl, monachus Ordinis

Order of St. Benedict, and
now at this present time
Abbot of the Monastery of
Brzewnow, in the diocese of
Prague — the said monas-
tery being *nullius,* free,
exempt, and immediately
subject to the Apostolic See
Provost of Wahlstad in
Silesia, mitred prelate of the
kingdom of Bohemia, and
perpetual Visitor of the said
Order in Bohemia, Moravia,
and Silesia—has recently
made known to Us, that on
another occasion he asked
of us for his successors, as
also for all and each of the
abbots, priors, and priests of
the said Order, who are or
shall be subject to him and
to his successors in the
office of Visitor, the faculty
to bless, according to the
formula given in the said
petition, the medals or
crosses called St. Bene-
dict's, and to distribute the
same respectively, in order

Sancti Benedicti expresse
professus, ac modernus
Abbas liberi et exempti,
Sedique Apostolicæ immediate subjecti monasterii
Brzevnoviensis in Brauna,
nullius, seu Pragensis
diœcesis, et Wahlstadii Silesiorum modernus Præposi-
tus, Prælatusque infulatus
regni Bohemiæ, dictique
Ordinis Visitator perpetuus
in Bohemia, Moravia et
Silesia: quod alias per Nos
eidem exponenti, ejusque
successoribus, ac omnibus
et singulis Abbatibus, Prioribus, cæterisque ejusdem
Ordinis monachis sacer-
dotibus, expetenti tamen
prædicto, ejusque successoribus Visitatoribus prædictis
subjectis, numismata seu
medallias, vel cruces, aut
cruculas Sancti Benedicti
nuncupatas, privativa facul-
tas, sub certa inibi expressa
formula benedicendi et respective distribuendi, pro

to spread the indulgences which have been so profusedly granted to them; with a prohibition to all ecclesiastics to interfere in this pious work: the which faculty was graciously accorded and imparted by a decree of the Congregation of Cardinals of the Holy Roman Church, called the Congregation of Indulgences, on the 23rd of the month of December, in the year of our Lord 1741, the text of which decree is as follows:

"*Decree for the Order of St. Benedict in Bohemia, Moravia, and Silesia:*

"At the most humble and instant entreaties of Dom Benno Löbl, Abbot of the free and exempt monastery of Brzewnow in Brauna, of the Order of St. Benedict, Provost of Wahlstad in Silesia, mitred prelate of the kingdom of

consequendis indulgentiis, in illis amplissime elargitis, cum inhibitione cuicumque personæ ecclesiasticæ in hujusmodi opere pio se immiscendi, decreto Congregationis Sanctæ Romanæ Ecclesiæ Cardinalium super indulgentiis præpositæ, sub die XXIII, mensis Decembris Anni Domini MDCCXLI emanato, benigne concessa et elargita fuit; cujus decreti tenor est qui sequitur:

"*Ordinis Sancti Benedicti per Bohemiam, Moraviam, et Silesiam Decretum:*

"Ad humillimas et enixas preces Domini Bennonis Löbl, Ordinis Sancti Benedicti, liberi et exempti Monasterii Brzevnoviensis in Brauna Abbatis, Wahlstadii Silesiorum Præpositi, regni Bohemiæ Prælati infulati, atque Ordinis prædicti

Bohemia, and perpetual Visitor of the said Order in Bohemia, Moravia, and Silesia: our most Holy Father Pope Benedict XIV has graciously given and granted to the same Benno, and to his successors, as also to all and each of the abbots, priors, and priests, who for the time being are subject to him as perpetual Visitor, the special faculty of blessing the medals, whether medals, properly so called, or medal crosses, called St. Benedict's, and of which one side represents the effigy of the same St. Benedict, and the other a cross, with these following letters or characters round the rim, which signify respectively as follows: V. *Vade*, R. *retro*, S. *Sathana*, N. *nunquam*, S. *suade*, M. *mihi*, V. *vana*, S. *sunt*, M. *mala*, Q. *quæ*, L. *libas*, I. *ipse*, V. *venena*, B. *bibas*. On the perpendicular line of the cross:

per Bohemiam, Moraviam, et Silesiam Visitatoris perpetui: Sanctissimus Dominus noster Benedictus PP. XIV., eidem Bennoni ejusque successoribus, ac omnibus et singulis Abbatibus, Prioribus, cæterisque monachis sacerdotibus, ipsimet pro tempore existenti Visitatori perpetuo subjectis, numismata, seu medallias, vel cruces aut cruculas Sancti Benedicti nuncupata, quarum una pars imaginem ejusdem Sancti Benedicti repræsentat, altera vero crucem, in cujus extremo circuitu litteræ seu characteres, scilicet: V. *Vade*, R. *retro*, S. *Satana*, N. *nunquam*, S. *suade*, M. *mihi*, V. *vana*, S. *sunt*, M. *mala*, Q. *quæ*, L. *libas*, I. *ipse*, V. *venena*, B. *bibas*. In linea vero ejus recta: C. *Crux*, S. *sacra*, S. *sit*, M. *mihi*, L. *lux*. In inversa autem: N. *Non*, D. *draco*, S. *sit*, M. *mihi*, D.

C. *crux,* S. *sacra,* S. *sit,* M. *mihi,* L. *lux.* On the horizontal line: N. *Non,* D. *draco,* S. *sit,* M. *mihi,* D. *dux.* Lastly, on the four corners, C. *Crux,* S. *Sancti,* P. *patris,* B. *Benedicti*; and the said blessing shall be in the formula as follows: *dux:* ac demum in quatuor lateribus, C. *Crux,* S. *Sancti,* P. *Patris,* B. *Benedicti,* respective significantes exprimuntur: facultatem privativam benedicendi, benigne concessit, atque indulsit, formula quæ sequitur, nimirum:

Adjutorium nostrum in nomine Domini. R. *Qui fecit cœlum et terram.*-Exorcizo vos numismata, per Deum Patrem ✠ omnipotentem, qui fecit cœlum et terram, mare et omnia quæ in eis sunt: omnis virtus adversarii, omnis exercitus diaboli, et omnis incursus, omne phantasma Satanæ eradicare et effugare ab his numismatibus, ut fiant omnibus, qui eis usuri sunt, salus mentis et corporis, in nomine Dei Patris ✠ omnipotentis, et Jesu Christi ✠ Filii ejus, Domini nostri, et Spiritus Sancti ✠ Paracliti, et in charitate ejusdem Domini nostri Jesu Christi, qui venturus est judicare vivos et mortuos et sæculum per ignem. *R. Amen.* Kyrie eleison, *Christe eleison,* Kyrie eleison. Pater noster, etc. *V.* Et ne nos inducas in tentationem.

R. Sed libera nos a malo. V. Salvos fac servos tuos.
R. Deus meus, sperantes in te. V. Esto nobis, Domine,
turris fortitudinis. *R. A facie inimici. V.* Deus virtutem
populo suo dabit. *R. Dominus benedicet populum
suum in pace. V.* Mitte eis, Domine, auxilium de
sancto. *R. Et de Sion tuere eos. V.* Domine, exaudi
orationem meam. *R. Et clamor meus ad te veniat. V.*
Dominus vobiscum. *R. Et cum Spiritu tuo.* Oremus.
Deus omnipotens, omnium bonorum largitor, supplices
te rogamus, ut per intercessionem Sancti Patris
Benedicti his sacris numismatibus litteris et
characteribus a te designates tuam benedictionem ✠
infundas, ut omnes, qui ea gestaverint, ac bonis
operibus intenti fuerint, sanitatem mentis et corporis,
et gratiam sanctificationis, atque indulgentias nobis
concessas consequi mereantur, omnesque diaboli
insidias et fraudes per auxilium misericordiæ tuæ
effugere valeant, et in conspectu tuo sancti et
immaculati appareant, per Dominum, etc., Oremus:
Domine Jesu, qui voluisti pro totius mundi
redemptione de Virgine nasci, circumcidi, a Judæis
reprobari, Judæ osculo tradi, vinculis alligari, spinis
coronari, clavis perforari, inter latrones crucifigi,
lancea vulnerari et tandem in cruce mori: per tuam
sanctissimam Passionem humiliter exoro, ut omnes
diabolicas insidias et fraudes expellas ab eo, qui
nomen sanctum tuum his litteris et characteribus a
te designatis devote invocaverit, et eum ad salutis
portum perducere digneris. Qui vivis et regnas, etc.

Benedictio Dei Patris ✠ omnipotentis, et Filii ✠, et Spiritus ✠ Sancti descendat super hæc numismata ac ea gestantes, et maneat semper. In nomine Patris ✠ et Filii ✠ et Spiritus ✠ Sancti. Amen. *Aspergatur aqua benedicta.*

"Being therefore desirous to enrich in a special manner, by spiritual favors and with the heavenly treasures of the Church, the aforesaid medals, blessed by the Visitor and the other monks mentioned above, for the time being, he has graciously given and granted to all and each of the faithful, of both sexes, who shall carry about their persons one of these medals or crosses thus blessed, and shall at the same time perform the good works which are enjoined as below in their respective places, the following indulgences in the manner and form as herein

"Eadem vero numismata sic per Visitatorem cæterosque monachos præfatos pro tempore existentes benedicta, et spiritualibus gratiis ac cœlestibus Ecclesiæ thesauris specialiter insignire volens: omnibus et singulis utriusque sexus Christi fidelibus, aliquod hujusmodi numismatum, seu crucularum, sic benedictum devote gestantibus, ac insimul pia opera, prout infra suis cuique locis respective injungitur, peragentibus, indulgentias modo et forma quæ præscribitur, clementer concessit atque indulsit, videlicet: ut qui saltem semel in

specified; to wit: he who shall regularly recite, at least once in the week, the chaplet of our Lord, or that of the most Blessed Virgin Mary, or the Rosary (or a third part of the Rosary), or the Divine Office, or the Little Office of the most Blessed Virgin Mary, or the Office of the Dead, or the Seven Penitential Psalms, or the Gradual Psalms or who shall regularly teach the rudiments of faith, or visit those who are in prison, or the sick in any hospital, or assist the poor, or either hear or, if he be a priest, say Mass; if he be truly penitent, and have confessed to a priest approved by the Ordinary, and have received the holy Sacrament of the Eucharist on any of the days following, namely: the feasts of the Nativity of our Lord Jesus

hebdomada Coronam Domini, vel Beatissimæ Virginis Mariæ, vel Rosarium, ejusve tertiam partem, aut Officium vel divinum, vel parvum ejusdem beatissimæ Virginis Mariæ, vel Defunctorum, aut septem Psalmos pœnientiales, vel Graduales, recitare, aut rudimenta fidei edocere, aut detentos in carcere, vel alicujus domus hospitalis ægrotos visitare, aut pauperibus subvenire, aut Missam vel audire, vel, si est sacerdos, celebrate consueverit; si vere pœnitens, et Sacerdoti per Ordinarium approbato confessus fuerit, ac sanctissimum Eucharistiæ sacramentum sumpserit, in quolibet ex diebus infra scriptis, nimirum: die festo Nativitatis Domini nostri Jesu Christi, Epiphaniæ, Resurrectionis, Ascensionis, Pentecostes, sanc-

Christ, Epiphany, Resurrection, Ascension, Pentecost, most Holy Trinity, and Corpus Christi, and on the feasts of the most Blessed Virgin Mary's Conception, Nativity, Annunciation, Purification, and Assumption; also on the first day of November, the feast of All Saints, and on the feast of St. Benedict; and   shall have devoutly prayed God for the destruction of heresies and schisms, for the exaltation and propagation of the Catholic faith, for the peace and concord of Christian princes, and for the other necessities of the Roman Church; he shall obtain a plenary indulgence and the remission of all his sins.

"He who shall have fulfilled the same said conditions on the other feasts of our Lord or of the most Blessed Virgin Mary,

tissimæ Trinitatis, et Corporis Christi, ac diebus Conceptionis, Nativitatis, Annuntiationis, Purificationis et Assumptionis Beatissimæ Virginis Mariæ; necnon primo die Novembris, festo Omnium Sanctorum, ac die festo Sancti Benedicti: et pro hæresum ac schismatum extirpatione, fidei catholicæ exaltatione ac propagatione, pace et christianorum principum concordia cæterisque Romanæ Ecclesiæ necessitatibus plas ad Deum preces effuderit, plenariam omnium peccatorum suorum remissionem et indulgentiam consequatur;

"Qui eadem in aliis festis Domini, aut Beatissimæ Virginis Mariæ, sanctorumque Apostolorum, aut Sancti Josephi, aut

and on the feasts of the Holy Apostles, or of St. Joseph, or of SS. Maurus, Placid, Scholastica, or Gertrude, of the Order of St. Benedict, shall gain on each of these feasts an indulgence of seven years and seven quarantines.

"Which same indulgence is also granted to him who shall hear, or, if he be a priest, shall say Mass, and shall pray God for the prosperity of Christian princes and for the tranquility of their states and possessions.

"He who shall fast on Fridays, out of reverence for the Passion of our Lord Jesus Christ, or on Saturdays, in honor of the most Blessed Virgin Mary, each day so fasting, he shall gain an indulgence of seven years and seven quarantines.

Sanctorum Mauri, Placidi, Scholasticæ, vel Gertrudis, Ordinis Sancti Benedicti, peregerit, in quolibet eorum septem annorum, totidemque quadragenarum indulgentiam acquirat.

"Quam pariter adipiscatur, qui Missam audiet, vel, si est sacerdos, celebrabit, ac pro christianorum principum prosperitate, illorumque statuum et ditionum tranquillitate Deum orabit.

"Qui ob reverentiam erga Passionem Jesu Christi Domini nostri, Feriis sextis, aut in honorem Beatissimæ Virginis Mariæ diebus Sabbati, jejunaverit, qualibet earum die id egerit, indulgentiam septem annorum, totidemque quadragenarum.

"And he who, having confessed and nourished himself with Holy Communion, shall have observed this same fast on the aforementioned days for one whole year, shall gain a plenary indulgence, which same also shall be granted to him who, having the intention of doing this same work, shall die within the year.

"He who shall have the custom of saying once or oftener in the day this ejaculation: *'Blessed be the most pure and Immaculate Conception of the most Blessed Virgin Mary'*, shall gain an indulgence of forty days.

"He who shall have the custom of reciting, at least once a week, the Chaplet or Rosary, or the Office of the most Blessed Virgin Mary, or the Office of the Dead, or the Vespers of the

"Qui vero confessus, ac sacra communione refectus, jejunium iisdem diebus per integrum annum, servaverit plenariam indulgentiam lucretur; qua etiam gaudeat qui idem opus complere intendens infra annum decesserit:

"Qui semel vel pluries in die jaculatoriam: *Benedicta sit purissima et Immaculata Conceptio Beatissimæ, Virgnis Mariæ,* proferre consueverit, indulgentiam quadraginta dierum acquirat.

"Qui saltem semel in hebdomada Coronam, aut Rosarium, aut Officium Beatissimæ Mariæ Virginis, vel Defunctorum, aut Vesperas cum uno saltem Nocturno et Laudibus, aut

Office of the Dead, with at least one Nocturn and Lauds, or the Seven Penitential Psalms, and the Litanies and their prayers, or five times the Lord's Prayer, either in honor of the most Holy Name of Jesus, or of His Five Wounds, of five times the Angelical Salutation or the Antiphon: *'We fly to thy patronage',* together with any one of the approved collects of the most Blessed Virgin, and this in honor of the most Holy Name of Mary, shall gain, on that day on which he does this, an indulgence of one hundred days; which same indulgence is likewise granted, once each Friday, to him who shall have thrice recited the Lord's Prayer, or the Angelical Salutation, and shall have piously meditated on the passion and

septem Psalmos Pœnitentiales et Litanias, earumque preces, aut in honorem sanctissimi Nominis Jesu, vel quinque ejus Plagarum, quinquies Orationem Dominicam, aut in honorem sanctissimi Nominis Mariæ quinquies Salutationem Angelicam, aut Antiphonam: *Sub tuum præsidium,* cum una qualibet ex approbatis Orationibus Beatissimæ Virginis recitare consueverit, quo die id egerit, indulgentiam centum dierum consequatur: qua semel in quavis Feria Sexta fruatur. Qui Orationem Dominicam ac Salutationem Angelicam ter dixerit, ac de Passione et morte Domini nostri Jesu Christi pie cogitaverit; eamdem pariter lucretur qui ob devotionem erga Sanctos Josephum, Benedictum, et Maurum, Scholasticam, ac Gertrudem, recitando Psalmum *Miser-*

death of our Lord Jesus Christ; which same also is granted to him who, out of devotion to St. Joseph, St. Benedict, St. Maurus, St. Scholastica, and St. Gertrude, shall recite the Psalm, *Miserere mei, Deus,* or five times the Lord's Prayer, or the Angelical Salutation, and shall pray God that He will, by their intercession, preserve the Holy Catholic Church, and give to himself a happy death.

"He who, in the celebration of Mass, or in Holy Communion, or in the recitation of the Divine Office, or of the Little Office of the most Blessed Virgin Mary, shall say some short prayer before he begins, shall receive fifty days' indulgence; which same is also granted to him who shall pray for those of the faithful who

ere mei, Deus, aut quinquies Orationem Dominicam et Salutationem Angelicam, oraverit ut Deus per eorum intercessionem, Sanctam Catholicam Ecclesiam conservet, ipsumque devotum beate fine quiescere faciat.

"Qui in celebranda Missa vel sumenda Eucharistia, aut Officio divino, vel parvo Beatissimæ Mariæ Virginis persolvendo, priusquam incipiat devotam aliquam precationem adhibuerit, quinquaginta dierum indulgentia gaudeat; quam similiter asequatur, qui pro Christi fidelibus in exitu vitæ constitutes Deum depreca-

are at the point of death, and shall say thrice, for their intention, the Lord's Prayer or the Angelical Salutation.

"He who shall visit those who are in prison, or the sick in hospitals, and shall assist them by any work of mercy, or shall teach Christian doctrine in the church or at home, either to children, or relations, or servants, each time, besides the indulgences granted for this by other Sovereign Pontiffs, such an one shall obtain also an indulgence of two hundred days.

"He who shall recite the Chaplet or the Rosary of the most Blessed Virgin Mary, in honor of her most pure and immaculate Conception, and shall ask her, by her intercession with her Divine Son, that he may live and die free

bitur, ac pro ipsis ter Orationem Dominicam et Salutationem Angelicam dixerit.

"Qui detentos in carcere, aut ægrotos in nosocomiis, eos aliquo pio opere adjuvando, visitaverit, aut doctrinam Christianam in ecclesia vel domi, filios aut propinquos, aut famulos docuerit, præter indulgentias ab aliis summis Pontificibus ad id concessas, toties indulgentiam bis centum dierum acquirat.

"Qui Coronam aut Rosarium Beatissimæ Mariæ Virginis in honorem ejusdem purissimæ et immaculatæ Conceptionis recitaverit, ipsam deprecans apud ejus Divinum Filium, ut sine lethali labe vivere et mori valeat, indul-

from mortal sin, shall receive an indulgence of seven years; which same indulgence is granted also to him, who shall devoutly accompany the most Holy Sacrament when carried as viaticum to the sick, and this over and above those other indulgences, which have been granted to the same pious act, by other Supreme Pontiffs.

"He who shall pray daily for the extirpation of heresies, shall gain, once each week, an indulgence of twenty years.

"He who shall examine his conscience and, being truly penitent, shall firmly resolve to correct himself of sins hitherto committed and confess them, shall gain, upon devoutly reciting the Lord's Prayer and the Angelical Salutation, one year's indulgence; and if he confess and receive

gentiam septem annorum percipiat; quam pariter qui sacratissimum Eucharistiæ viaticum ad infirmos devote sociaverit, præter indulgentias ad idem tam pium opus ab aliis Summis Pontificibus concessas, omnino consequatur.

"Qui quotidie pro hæresum extirpatione oraverit, indulgentiam viginti annorum semel in hebdomada lucretur.

"Qui conscientiam suam excusserit, ac vere pœnitens peccata commissa emendare et confiteri firmiter proposuerit, quinquies Oratione Dominica et Salutatione Angelica devote repetita, unius anni; si vero confessus, et sacra communione refectus fuerit, eadem die decem annorum indulgentia fruatur.

Holy Communion, he shall gain an indulgence of ten years that same day.

"He who shall, by his good example or advice, lead any sinner to repentance, shall obtain the remission of one third of the punishment in what way soever due to his sins; and he who, being truly penitent, shall go to confession and Holy Communion on Holy Thursday, and Easter Sunday, and shall devoutly pray to God for the exaltation of our Holy Mother the Church, and for the preservation of the Sovereign Pontiff, shall gain those same indulgences which His Holiness grants, on the said days, in giving his solemn blessing to the people.

"He who shall beseech God to propagate the Order of St. Benedict, shall become partaker of all and

"Qui probo suo exemplo aut consilio aliquem peccatorem ad pœnitentiam reduxerit, tertiæ partis pœnarum sibi propter sua peccata alias quomodolibet debitarum remissionem consequatur; qui vere pœnitens confessus, sacraque communione refectus in Feria quinta Cœnæ Domini, et in die Paschalis Resurrectionis, pro Sanctæ Matris Ecclesiæ exaltatione, Summique Pontificis conservatione, pias ad Deum preces effuderit, easmet acquirat indulgentias quas iisdem diebus Sanctitas Sua populo benedicens publice elargitur.

"Qui Deum pro Ordinis seu religionis Sancti Benedicti propagatione deprecatus fuerit, particeps fit

each of the good works which in any manner whatsoever are done in the said Order.

"He who by reason of bodily infirmity, or other lawful impediment, is not able to hear, or, being priest, to say Mass, or to say either the Divine Office, or that of the most Blessed Virgin Mary, or has it not in his power to perform the other exercises of piety which are enjoined for obtaining the aforesaid indulgences, shall, notwithstanding, receive the same on thrice saying, in the place of the said pious exercises, the Lord's Prayer, and the Angelical Salutation, and the anthem, *Salve Regina,* adding at the end, *'Blessed be the most Holy Trinity, and praised be the most Holy Sacrament, and the Conception of the*

omnium et singulorum bonorum operum, quæ in eadem Religione quomodolibet peraguntur.

"Qui vel infirmitate corporis, vel alio legitimo impedimento detentus, Missam audire, aut si est sacerdos, celebrare, aut Officium vel Divinum, vel Beatissimæ Mariæ Virginis, aut alia virtutis exercitia, ad prædictas indulgentias acquirendas injuncta peragere nequiverit, iisdem nihilominus gaudeat, si pro ipsis piis exercitiis recitaverit ter Orationem Dominicam et Salutationem Angelicam ac Antiphonam: *Salve, Regina.* Atque in fine ipsius dixerit: *Benedicta sit sanctissima Trinitas, et laudetur Sanctissimum Sacramentum, ac Conceptio Beatissimæ, Virginis Mariæ sine labe conceptæ,* dummodo tamen confessus ac sacra

Most Blessed Virgin Mary, conceived without sin;' provided, nevertheless, that he shall have been to confession and Holy Communion, or at least shall have contrition for his sins, and the firm resolution of afterwards confessing them.

"He who, being at the point of death, shall devoutly recommend his soul to God, and having previously gone to confession and received Holy Communion, if he have it in his power, or, if not, having made from his heart an act of contrition, shall, with his lips, or, if he cannot do more, at least in his heart, invoke the names of Jesus and Mary, shall obtain a plenary indulgence and remission of all his sins.

"Each one may gain for himself, or apply, by man-

communione refectus fuerit, vel saltem contritus inde sua peccata confiteri firmiter proposuerit.

"Qui in articulo mortis animam suam Deo pie commendans præmissa peccatorum suorum confessione, sumptaque sanctissima Eucharistia, si potuerit: si minus, elicita cordis contritione, Jesu et Mariæ nomina ore, si potuerit; si alioquin, corde saltem invocaverit, plenariam omnium peccatorum suorum remissionem et indulgentiam consequatur.

"Quilibet omnes et singulas prædictas indulgentias

ner of suffrage, to the faithful departed, all and each of the aforesaid indulgences, as also the remission of sins and the relaxation of the punishments thereunto due.

"Notwithstanding anything whatsoever to the contrary, His Holiness has declared that the medals herein mentioned, which shall not have been blessed by the monks aforesaid, or by those to whom the Holy See has, by a special favor, granted the power, shall in nowise be indulgenced. He has also forbidden that the said medals should be of paper, or such-like material; and that unless they be made of gold, silver, brass, copper, or other solid metal, they shall not be indulgenced.

"In all things relating to the distribution and use of

ac peccatorum remissiones, necnon pœnitentiarum relaxationes, aut ipse pro se adipici, aut fidelibus defunctis per modum suffragii applicare valeat.

"Non obstantibus quibuscumque in contrarium facientibus, Sanctitas Sua declaravit, quod ejusmodi numismata seu medalliæ, quæ non fuerint benedictæ a præfatis monachis, vel quibus ab Apostolica Sede ex speciali gratia indultum fuerit, omni penitus indulgentia careant. Item vetuit ejusmodi medallias chartaceas, vel ex simili materia confectas, sed tantummodo ex auro, argento, ære, auricalcho, aliove solido metallo consistentes; aliter nulla prorsus gaudeant indulgentia.

"In distribuendis hujusmodi numismatibus, eo-

the said medals, His Holiness moreover orders, that there should be observed the decree of Alexander VII, of happy memory, published on the 6th day of February 1657, to wit: that medals blessed and indulgenced as here mentioned, cannot pass beyond the persons to whom, either the said monks shall have given them, or to whom they shall have been by them distributed in the first instance; neither can they be lent, nor sold, nor borrowed without their losing the indulgences which have been attached to them; and if one be lost, another cannot be taken in its place, unless it have been blessed by those before mentioned, notwithstanding any concession or privilege to the contrary.

"Moreover, His Holi-

rumque usu, eadem

Sanctitas Sua servari jubet Decretum felicis recordationis Alexandri VII, editum sub die Sexta Februarii MDCLVII, nimirum, ut numismata, quæ vulgo medalliæ nuncupantur, cum prædictis indulgentiis benedicta non transeant personam illorum, quibus a monarchis prædictis concedentur, aut quibus ab eis prima vice distribuentur, nec commodari aut vendi, aut precario dari valeant; alioquin careant indulgentiis jam concessis; et aliqua deperdita, altera pro ea subrogari nullo modo possit, nisi a quibus supra benedicta fuerit; quacumque concessione, aut privilegio in contrarium non obstante.

"Insuper expresse pro-

ness expressly forbids any priest, whether secular, or of any Order, Congregation, or regular Institute whatsoever, and whatsoever may be his dignity or office, with the exception of the monks here abovementioned, or of those to whom the Holy See shall, by a special privilege, have granted the faculty, to dare or presume to bless the said medals or crosses, or to distribute them to the faithful after having so blessed them, under such penalties, besides the nullity of the blessing and indulgences, as it shall seem good to the respective Ordinaries, or Inquisitors of the faith to inflict, according to the gravity of the fault. Notwithstanding all things soever which may be to the contrary, these presents shall hold good

hibet ne quis sacerdos, sive sæcularis, sive cujus libet Ordinis, Congregationis, aut Instituti regularis, quavis etiam dignitate aut officio insignitus, extra prædictos monachos, vel quibus a Sancta Sede ex speciali privilegio indultum fuerit, ejusmodi numismata, seu cruces, ut prædicitur, benedicere, aut a se benedicta fidelibus distribuere audeat, vel præ sumat, sub pœnis, præter nullitatem benedictionis et indulgentiarum, per respectivos locorum Ordinarios aut fidei Inquisitores, juxta reatus qualitatem, arbitrio infligendis. Quibuscumque in contrarium facientibus non obstantibus, præsentibus perpetuis futuris temporibus valituris.

unto all future times.

"His Holiness likewise has willed that the copy of these present letters, whether in manuscript or printing, when signed by a public notary, or by the secretary of the fore-mentioned perpetual Visitor, now at this present in office, sealed also with the seal of some dignitary, or of the fore-mentioned Benno, or of the perpetual Visitor for the time being, shall have the same weight in all questions of dispute or otherwise, and in all places, which would be given to these presents on their being shown or produced.

"Given at Rome, the 23rd day of December, the year 1741.

(The Seal.) L. Cardinal PICO, Prefect.

A. M. ERBA, Apostolic Protonotary, Secretary of

"Voluitque Sanctitas Sua, quod istarum litterarum transsumptis, seu exemplis, etiam impressis, alicujus notarii publici, vel secretarii Visitatoris perpetui prædicti, pro tempore existentis, subscriptis, et sigillo personæ in dignitate constituæ, aut ejusdem Bennonis, aut existentis pro tempore Visitatoris perpetui munitis eadem prorsus in judicio, et extra ubique locorum, fides adhibeatur quæ haberetur eis præsentibus; si forent exhibitæ vel ostensæ.

"Datum Romæ, die XXIII Decembris, anno MDCCXLI.

(L. S.) L. Cardinalis PICUS, Præfectus.

A. M. ERBA, Protonotarius Apostolicus,

the Sacred Congregation.

But although, as the same Petition added, no one could doubt of the validity of this decree and of the said faculty, nevertheless, to procure for them with all persons, greater respect and authority, the said petitioner, greatly desiring that this decree, with all things therein contained and expressed, should be approved, and for ever confirmed, by Us and the Apostolic See, as we are here about to do, has humbly sent to us a petition and earnest entreaty, that we would be pleased to grant him by Apostolic favor and by these presents, that which he asks of us.

We, therefore, wishing to show to the said petitioner a mark of our

Sacræ Congregationis Secretarius.

Sed etsi, sicut eadem expositio subjungebat, de hujusmodi Decreti, dictæque facultatis validitate hæsitari non possit; attamen cum pro ejusdem majori apud omnes veneratione et validiori illius subsistentia, dictus exponens plurimum cupiat, Decretum prædictum cum omnibus et singulis in eo contentis et expressis, per Nos et Sedem Apostolicam ut infra, perpetuo approbari et confirmari; ideo nobis humiliter supplicari fecit expressis petens, ut ei in præsentibus opportune providere de benignitate Apostolica dignaremur.

Nos igtur eumdem exponentem specialis gratæ favore prosequi volentes,

special favor, and declaring him to be loosed and absolved, for the sole intent of his obtaining the effect of these presents, from all excommunication, suspension, and interdict, and other ecclesiastical sentences by whomsoever pronounced, as also from all censures and punishments, *a jure* or *ab homine,* on whatsoever occasion or for whatsoever cause awarded, in case he were under any such; determined thereunto by the supplications which he has unto this purpose addressed to us, we approve and confirm by our Apostolical authority, by the tenor of these presents for ever, the aforementioned Decree, with all it contains and expresses; and thereto we add the inviolable strength of the Apostolical confirmation,

necnon a quibusvis excommunicationis, suspensionis et interdicti, aliisque ecclesiasticis sententiis, censuris et pœnis a jure, vel ab homine, quavis occasione vel causa latis, si quibus quomodolibet innodatus existit, ad effectum præsentium tantum consequendum, earum serie absolvendum et absolutum fore censentes, hujusmodi supplicationibus inclinati, Decretum prædictum cum omnibus et singulis in eo contentis et expressis, Apostolica auctoritate, tenore præsentium perpetuo approbamus et confirmanus, illique inviolabile Apostolicæ firmitatis robur adjicimus, omnesque et singulos tam juris quam facti et solemnitatum, aliosque quantumvis substantiales defectus, si qui desuper quomodolibet interveniunt, in eisdem sup-

making good all and each of such defects, whether of fact, or right, or formality, or of any other kind soever, even though they were substantial, which may be in these same. We wish that these present letters be, and continue forever, firm, valid, and of effect, and that they receive their full and entire effects. We declare that they shall not be comprised in the revocations, limitations, derogations, or other contrary decisions, which have been, or shall hereafter be made by Us, and the Roman Pontiffs, in reference to such favors as these or to any favors whatsoever; but that these same shall be always excepted, and shall as often as the aforesaid revocations be made, be each time restored, replaced, and fully re-estab-

plemus; necnon præsentes litteras semper et perpetuo firmas, validas et efficaces esse et fore, suosque plenarios et integros effectus sortiri et obtinere; nec illas sub quibusvis similium vel dissimilium gratiarum revocationibus, suspensionibus, limitationibus, derogationibus, aut aliis contrariis dispositionibus, per Nos et Romanos Pontifices successores nostros pro tempore factis et faciendis, comprehendi, sed semper ab illis excipi, et quoties illæ emanabunt, toties in pristinum et validissimum statum restitutas, repositas, et plenary reintegratas; ac denuo etiam sub quacumque posteriori data per exponentem, ejusque successores prædictos quandocumque eligendos, concessas fore et esse, suosque plenarios effectus sortiri et obtinere,

lished to and in their former and most valid state: and lastly, we wish that under what later date soever they be communicated by the petitioner, and by his successors hereafter to be elected, they receive their full effect, and that neither the petitioner nor his successors be disturbed, molested, or impeded, by any authority, or under any pretext, color, or pretence whatsoever. Thus, and in no other way, must it be judged and defined by all persons exercising any authority whatsoever, ordinary or delegated, even by the Auditors of causes of the Apostolic Palace, by the Cardinals of the Holy Roman Church, even should they be Legates *a latere,* and the Nuncios of the Holy See. We declare null and void whatsoever shall

eumdemque exponentem propterea, et successores suos prædictos super præsentibus omnibus et singulis a quoquam quavis auctoritate fungente, quovis prætextu, colore, vel ingenio perturbari, inquietari, aut quoquo modo impediri posse, neque debere; sicque et non aliter per quoscunque Ordinarios vel delegatos quavis auctoritate fungentes, etiam causarum Palatii Apostolici Auditores, ac Sanctæ Romanæ Ecclesiæ Cardinales, etiam de latere Legatos dictæque Sedis Nuncios, judicari et definiri debere: irritum quoque et inane decernimus, si super eis a quoquam, quavis auctoritate, scienter vel ignoranter contigerit attentari; non obstantibus Constitutionibus et ordinationibus Apostolicis, dictique Ordinis, etiam juramento,

be attempted contrary to the aforesaid letters, by any one whomsoever, by any authority whatsoever, whether this be done with or without knowledge. And all this notwithstanding the Apostolical constitutions and rules, as well as those of the said Order, even, were they strengthened by Apostolic attestation, confirmation, or any other support; notwithstanding likewise all statutes, customs, privileges, Apostolic letters, granted, confirmed, and renewed to all superiors and others, which should be in anywise contrary to the said privileges. From all and each of the which constitutions and rules we hereby derogate, as likewise from all other expressions to the contrary, even in those cases where it would be required to make mention or any other

confirmatione Apostolica vel quavis firmitate alia roboratis, statutis et consuetudinibus, privilegiis quoque indultis, litteris Apostolicis, quibusvis superioribus et personis in contrarium privilegiorum quomodolibet facientibus, concessis, confirmatis et innovatis; quibus omnibus et singulis, etiamsi de illis eorumque totis tenoribus specialis, et specifica, expressa et individua, non autem per alias generales idem importantes, mentio seu quævis alia expressio habenda, aut aliqua alia exquisita forma ad hoc servanda foret; eorum tenores, etiamsi de verbo ad verbum, nihil penitus omisso, et forma in illis tradita observata, inserti forent; præsentibus pro expressis habendis, illis alias in suo robore permansuris, latissime et

expression of them, specially and specifically, express and formal, even by the insertion of the whole tenor, and not by a general and virtual mention; as likewise in such cases as would require that they should be expressed word for word, without any single omission, and in the form in which they are usually drawn up; the said constitutions, rules, and the like, which are to be considered as expressed in these presents, and are otherwise to remain in full vigor, are hereby derogated from most largely and fully in this particular case, whatever may, in any way, be to the contrary.

Given at Rome, at St. Mary Major's, under the Fisherman's Seal, the 12th of March 1742, the second year of our Pontificate.

plenissime, hac vice duntaxat derogamus, et cæteris contrariis quibuscumque.

Datum Romæ, apud Sanctam Mariam Majorem, sub annulo Piscatoris, die duodecima Martii MDCCXLII pontificatus nostri anno secundo.

The Cardinal Prodatary.   P. Cardinalis Prod.

CHAPTER XII

CONSEQUENCES OF THE BRIEF OF BENEDICT XIV
IN REGARD TO THE MEDAL OF ST. BENEDICT

It follows, in the first place, from the Papal document
which we have just given, that the medal of St. Benedict
is put under the sanction of the Holy See. The pretended
scruples which certain persons had excited   regarding
it, are hereby shown to be groundless. It is well known
with what extreme caution, and with what profound knowledge of principles, Rome proceeds in everything. She has
not, however, found anything superstitious in this medal;
the letters which are marked upon it have not seemed
to her deserving of the slightest suspicion. The using
of the first letter of a word for the word itself may have
appeared strange to the author mentioned above (Chap.
XI), who, like so many other intolerant critics of his time,
had but a very shallow knowledge of archeology otherwise he would no more have thought it strange to express these words, *Vade retro*, *Satana*, *etc.*, by V. R. S.,
etc., than it is to employ, as did the early Christians, the

word Ἰχθὺς, to stand for these words, of which it contains the initials, Ἰησοῦς Χριστος Θεοῦ ᾑος Σωτηρ.[1] At Rome, these things have always been perfectly understood, and the approbation of St. Benedict's medal, with its inscription, which is so easily explained, could not meet with the slightest opposition from any fear of appearing to be giving a sanction to some superstitious formula.

But the approbation is given not only to the medal, but also to the prayers to be used in blessing it. Moreover, a liberal grant of indulgences is made to all who shall wear it or carry it about them with devotion. We give in the next chapter the list of these indulgences, with the conditions for gaining them, as specified in the Papal Brief. It is clear, therefore, that the Holy See formally recommends the medal or cross of St. Benedict, to the confidence of the faithful.

The privilege of blessing the medal and attaching the indulgences to it is, as we have just seen, reserved to the Benedictines of Bohemia, Moravia, and Silesia, with a strict prohibition to any other priest, unless he

---

[1] The initial letters of the phrase Ἰησοῦς Χριστος Θεοῦ ᾑος Σωτηρ, form the Greek word Ἰχθὺς, a *fish*. Hence among the early Christians a fish was an emblem of the Son of God, our Lord Jesus Christ, as the *lamb*, is amongst us now. We learn this from many representations in the Catacombs. Hence several of the Fathers, commenting on those passages of the Holy Gospels where Christ gives His apostles or the people *fish* to eat, make that act figurative of His giving Himself to us as our food in the Blessed Sacrament. (See "Spicilegium, etc.," by Card. Pitra, O.S.B.) —ED.

has received permission, to exercise this privilege, under penalty of nullity both to the blessing and the indulgences. This same power has been since extended to the various Congregations of the Order of St. Benedict.[1] With regard to the approved form of blessing, it is of strict obligation; so that it would not be enough to make use of the simple sign of the cross, as is generally done in the attaching indulgences to medals, crosses, and beads, in virtue of faculties granted by the Holy See.

In case, however, of any one not being able to meet with a priest who has the faculty to bless the medal of St. Benedict, a Christian may still have confidence in this sacred object. Of course, it deserves our confi-

[1] His Holiness, Gregory XVI, extended to the Congregation of Monte Cassino all the privileges that had been granted by Benedict XIV to the Benedictines of Bohemia and other countries; and the late Sovereign Pontiff, Pius IX, by an audience, March 18, 1855, has conferred them on all priests of the English Benedictine Congregation, as may be seen from the following:

"De Numismate SS. P. N.

"Beatissimo Padre,—Il P.D. Paulino Heptonstall, Provincial della Congregazione Anglo-Benedettina, supplica umilmente la Santità Vostra per ottinere alla sua Congregazione la medesima facolta accordata alla Congregazione Cassinese di benedire coll' Indulgenze annesse le Medaglie di S. Benedetto. *Che della grazia, etc.*

"Ex audientia SSmi, 18 Mart. 1855.

"S. Smus Dnus N. Pius divina providentia P.P. IX, referente me infrascripto S.C. de Propaganda Fide Secretario, benigne annuit pro gratia juxta petita per rescriptum præfatæ Cong. absque ulla brevis expeditione. Contrariis non obstantibus. Datum Romæ ex æd. S.C. die at anno prædictis. Gratis, etc.

"AL. BARNABO, a Secretis." —ED.

dence so much the more, when it has been enriched with the blessings of the Church, and with the indulgences which she grants to those who carry it about their persons. At the same time, we must not forget that many favours were obtained by its means, even before it had been made the object of such special privileges, as we have seen bestowed on it by the Holy See. The power of the medal is attached to the sign of the cross, which is marked on it, and to the effigy of St. Benedict, whose protection is secured to those who wear it.

The Holy Name of Jesus, the words which our Saviour made use of in driving the devil away, and the allusion to the victories of St. Benedict over this spirit of evil, are all so many holy forms of exorcism which the fiend cannot withstand when they are used against him with faith.

Whilst, therefore, recommending the faithful to do their utmost to get their medals blessed, we must remind them that they ought to make use of it, and have confidence in the Holy Cross and St. Benedict, even when they have no opportunity of having it blessed by a priest who has the necessary power.

The reader has seen in the Brief that the effigy of St. Benedict is necessary for the medal. It is not there-fore enough that there be engraven on it the letters C. S. P. B. (*Crux Sancti Patris Benedicti*); it must, moreo-ver, have upon it the effigy of the holy Patriarch of the Monks of the West. There have been, within the last few years, a great number of medals made in France, which have not the effigy of St. Benedict upon them; these cannot be blessed as medals of the Saint, and they are essentially different from those which have been made both before and after the Brief of Pope Benedict XIV. It is well to make the faithful aware of this, and to impress upon them that these other medals, in spite of their being widely circulated in some places, are not authentic. The medal has been, from its first beginning, consecrated to the honour of the Holy Cross and St. Benedict; both have always been represented on it from its very beginning, and it is only under this special form that the Church offers it to her children.

As one cannot dispense with the effigy of St. Benedict without essentially changing the medal, so precisely for the same reason, it is wrong to put anything else whatsoever upon it. We must consequently consider as spurious certain medals struck off in Germany. They are of a large size, and bear a device expressive of their being medals of St. Zachary. This medal is quite distinct from that of St. Benedict which is the subject of these pages. It is true, it has upon it the effigy of the holy Patriarch, and eighteen letters are written round the medal, which, if they mean anything at all, must be the initials of as many words, like the Ἰχθὺς of the early Christians, or the abjurations inscribed, by their initials, on the medal of St. Benedict.

Some have endeavoured to explain these eighteen letters by making them the initials of a series of formulas, in which God is besought to deliver us from pestilence. To say the least of it, it is strange that one single letter should be made to stand for a whole sentence, and this sentence sometimes a long one; thus, for instance, there is one which is composed of fifty-one words. This explanation, which is arbitrary from beginning to end, gives us a collection of sentences which have no connection whatever with each other. And then, why is there the figure of St. Benedict upon this medal? Not the slightest allusion is made to the Saint in the explanation given to the eighteen letters; whereas on the true medal everything which does not allude to the holy cross refers to the holy Patriarch. It may reasonably be doubted whether the Holy See would ever consent to give its approval to an object of so confused and undetermined a character. The propagators of this medal would have it that its originator was the holy Pope Zachary, who began his reign in the year 741; but so far they have not been able to give the merest shadow of a proof for such an assertion. In saying this we have no intention of hurting the feelings of any one; but it seemed necessary to make these few observations relative to a medal which would justify, by its strange pretensions, the severity of criticism, and indirectly bring discredit and disrespect to the true medal of St. Benedict.

We must also protest against an error which is found upon a very great number of the medals of St. Benedict which are distributed. A gross ignorance of the habits of the different Religious Orders has given rise to this error, which represents the figure of St. Benedict in a dress, which is not that of his Order. On some of these medals we find, for instance, the holy Patriarch muffled in a cloak which is girded at the waist by a cord, after the manner of the Franciscans, instead of his having on the cowl, which is the essentially distinctive habit of the Benedictine. Not that such an error invalidates the medals, but it is one which ought to be corrected. The emblems or attributes which ecclesiastical tradition has assigned to each Saint, cannot be set aside without a sort of irreverence, and the caprice or ignorance of artists who do so, ought not to be tolerated. The impressions of the medal which we are now alluding to, are fortunately beginning to get rare, and the sooner the better; for besides their giving the wrong habit, they represent St. Benedict in anything but a chaste style.

The medals which are now in circulation are much more correct, and one has just been struck off in Paris, which is perhaps the best of all that have yet appeared; it is of several sizes.[1]

---

[1] Currently (2002) the St. Benedict Medal and Medal-Crosses can be obtained from Saint Benedict Priory, P.O. Box 49, Still River, MA 01467-0049. —Publishers note.

CHAPTER XIII

We have thought it would be well, for the convenience of our readers, to give a list of all the indulgences granted by the Holy See to those who make use of the medal of St. Benedict. It is not easy to distinguish them as they are given in the Brief of Benedict XIV. We will classify them into the two ordinary divisions, *plenary* and *partial*.

I. Those who devoutly carry about their persons the medal of St. Benedict, may gain a *plenary indulgence* on the following festivals:

Christmas Day
Epiphany
Easter Sunday
Ascension Day
Whit Sunday
Trinity Sunday

Corpus Christi
The Immaculate Conception
The Nativity of Our Lady
The Annunciation
The Purification
The Assumption
All Saints' Day
St. Benedict's (21st of March)

Besides the usual conditions of confession and Holy Communion, and praying, according to the intentions of the Sovereign Pontiff, it is requisite, in order to gain the above-mentioned indulgences, that one should perform habitually, that is to say, once at least in the week, one of the following pious practices:

Recite the Chaplet of our Lord or the Rosary,
Or a third part of the Rosary,
Or the Divine Office,
Or the Little Office of Our Lady,
Or the Office of the Dead,
Or the Seven Penitential Psalms,
Or the Gradual Psalms;
Teach the rudiments of faith to children or the poor;
Visit those who are in prison,
Or those who are sick in hospitals;
Give relief to the poor;
Hear Mass or; if a priest, say Mass.

II. A *Plenary indulgence* to him who, being at the point of death, after having made his confession and received Holy Communion, if he be able, or, if not, after having made from his heart an act of contrition, shall devoutly recommend his soul to God, and shall invoke with his lips, or, if he cannot do more, at least in his heart, the Holy Names of Jesus and Mary.

III. A *plenary indulgence*, the same as that which is given by the Sovereign Pontiff by the Papal benediction at St. Peter's of the Vatican on Maundy Thursday and Easter Sunday, is granted to him who, being truly penitent, having confessed his sins and received Holy Communion on those two same days, shall pray devoutly for the exaltation of Holy Church, and for the preservation of the Supreme Pontiff.

IV. The indulgence and remission of a *third part* of the punishment due to his sins to him who, by his good example and advice, shall lead a sinner to repentance.

V. An indulgence of *twenty years*, once each week, to him who shall daily pray for the extirpation of heresies.

VI. An indulgence of *seven years and seven quarantines*[1] to him who shall perform the several pious works specified in No. I. on the lesser feasts of our Lord and of our Lady; for example, the Circumcision, the Holy Name of Jesus, the Transfiguration, etc.; the Visitation of the most Blessed Virgin, her Presentation, her Seven Dolours, the Holy Rosary, etc. The same indulgence, on the same conditions, for the feasts of St. Joseph, spouse of the most Holy Virgin, of St. Maurus St. Placid, St. Scholastica, and St. Gertrude.

---

[1] A quarantine indulgence is equivalent to the remission of so much temporal punishment due to sin, as would equal forty days fasting on bread and water.

Vll. An indulgence of *seven years and seven quarantines* to him who shall hear, or, if he be a priest, shall celebrate Mass, and pray for the prosperity of Christian princes and for the tranquillity of their states.

VIII An indulgence of *seven years and seven quarantines* each time, to him who, out of devotion to the Passion of our Lord Jesus Christ, shall fast on Fridays, or in honour of the Blessed Virgin Mary on Saturdays. He who shall have performed either of these two fasts during a whole year, shall gain a *plenary indulgence* on a day of his choice, when, having made his confession, he shall receive Holy Communion. Should he happen to die during the course of the year, during which he had the intention of keeping up this pious practice, he shall obtain the same indulgence.

IX. An indulgence of *seven years and seven quarantines* to him who shall say the Rosary or Chaplet, in honour of the Immaculate Conception of the most Holy Virgin Mary, beseeching her to intercede with her Divine Son, to obtain for him the grace of living and dying without committing a mortal sin.

X. An indulgence of *seven years and seven quarantines* to him who shall accompany the most Holy Sacrament when carried to the sick. This indulgence is in addition to those already granted by the Supreme Pontiffs to the faithful who practise this devotion.

XI. An indulgence of *one year* to him who, having examined his conscience, and being truly penitent for his sins, shall be resolved to avoid them for the future and to confess them, and shall say five Paters and five Aves. If he go to confession and receive Holy Communion, he shall on that day gain an indulgence of *ten years*.

XII. An indulgence of *two hundred days* to him who shall visit those who are in prison, or those who are sick in hospitals, rendering to them some service of charity; the same is granted to him who shall teach Christian doctrine, or, as it is called, catechism, either in the church or at home, to his children, neighbours, or servants.

XIII. An indulgence of *one hundred days* to him who, on Fridays, shall devoutly meditate on the Passion and Death of our Lord, and say three times the Lord's Prayer and the Angelical Salutation.

XIV. An indulgence of one hundred days to him who, out of devotion to St. Joseph, St. Benedict, St. Maurus, St. Scholastica, or St. Gertrude, shall say the psalm *Miserere*, or five Paters and five Aves, begging of God that He will, by the intercession of these His Saints, preserve the Holy Catholic Church, and grant him a happy death.

XV. An indulgence of one hundred days to him who has the habit of saying, at least once in the week, the holy Rosary or Chaplet, or the Office of our Lady, or that of the Dead, or only the Vespers and one Nocturn and Lauds of the same Office, or the seven Penitential Psalms, with the Litany of the Saints and the prayers which follow it; or five Paters and five Aves, in honour of the most Holy Name of Jesus or of his Five Wounds;

or five Aves, or the Antiphon, *We fly to thy Patronage, etc.,* with one of the approved collects, in honour of the most Holy Name of Mary.

XVI. An indulgence of *fifty days* to him who, before saying Mass, going to Holy Communion, reciting the Divine Office or the Little Office of our Lady, shall say some devout prayer.

XVII. An indulgence of *fifty days* to him who shall pray for those who are in their last agony, and shall say for their intention three Paters and three Aves.

XVIII. An indulgence of *forty days* to him who shall say, once or oftener during the day, this ejaculatory prayer, *"Blessed be the most pure and Immaculate Conception of the Blessed Virgin Mary."*

XIX. He who shall pray God to spread the Order of St. Benedict shall enter into a participation of all and each of the good works, of what kind soever, which are done by that Order.

XX. He who through sickness, or any other lawful impediment, cannot hear, or, being a priest, cannot say, Mass, nor recite either the Divine Office or the Office of Our Lady, nor, in fine, perform the other acts of virtue enjoined for the gaining the above indulgences, may supply them by reciting three Paters and three Aves, followed by the anthem, *Salve Regina, etc.,* adding to these prayers the following aspiration, *"Blessed be the most Holy Sacrament, and the Conception of the Most Blessed Virgin Mary, conceived without sin!"* If the indulgence intended to be gained be a plenary one, it is necessary to confess one's sins and receive Holy Communion. But should one not have it in his power to do this, he must at least be contrite in his heart, and be firmly resolved to confess his sins when opportunity serves.

All the indulgences here mentioned are applicable to the souls in Purgatory.[1]

The Decree expressly forbids the selling of the medals after the indulgences have been attached to them; as also the lending of them to other persons, for the purpose of communicating the indulgences.

It also reminds the faithful, that in case a person loses an indulgenced medal, and procures another in its place without having had the indulgences attached to it by a priest who has the power, such a person does not enjoy the same favours as those who have had their medal properly blessed.

[1] Many new indulgences besides these, are attached to the medal struck at Monte Cassino to commemorate the fourteenth centenary of St. Benedict. (See Appendix.) —ED.

CHAPTER XIV

RITE TO BE USED IN BLESSING
THE MEDAL OF ST. BENEDICT

We have seen in the Brief of Pope Benedict XIV the formula of exorcisms and prayers to be used by the priest, empowered to bless the medals for the indulgences which are granted to them, and which we have just enumerated. This formula was presented to the Holy See by Benno Löbl, Abbot of St. Margaret's of Prague; and the sacred Congregation of Indulgences, after having made some few changes in it, approved of it by its Decree dated December 23, 1741. We have thought it would be useful to give this blessing, according to the copy printed at Monte Cassino in the year 1844.

Sacerdos professus Ordinis S. Benedicti et Privilegio fruens, indutus stola, ante se habens numismata benedicenda, incipit absolute.

V. Adjutorium nostrum in nomine Domini.

R. Qui fecit cælum et terram.

Exorcizo vos, numismata, per Deum Patrem ✠ omnipotentem, qui fecit cœlum et terram, mare et omnia quæ in eis sunt. Omnis virtus adversarii, omnis exercitus diaboli et omnis incursus, omne phantasma Satanæ, eradicare et effugare ab his numismatibus, ut fiant omnibus qui eis usuri sunt salus mentis et corporis, in nomine Dei Patris ✠ omnipotentis, et Jesu ✠ Christi Filii ejus Domini nostri, et Spiritus ✠ Sancti Paracliti et in charitate ejusdem Domini nostri Jesu Christi qui venturus est judicare vivos et mortuos et sæculum per ignem.

R. Amen.

Kyrie éleison.
Christe éleison.
Kyrie éleison.
Pater noster.
V. Et ne nos inducas in tentationem.
R. Sed libera nos a malo.
V. Salvos fac servos tuos.
R. Deus meus, sperantes in te.
V. Esto nobis, Domine, turris fortitudinis.
R. A facie inimici.
V. Deus virtutem populo suo dabit.
R. Dominus benedicet populum suum in pace.
V. Mitte eis, Domine, auxilium de Sancto.
R. Et de Sion tuere eos.
V. Domine, exaudi orationem meam.
R. Et clamor meus ad te veniat.

V. Dominus vobiscum.

R. Et cum spiritu tuo.

Deus omnipotens, bonorum omnium largitor, supplices te rogamus, ut per intercessionem sancti Patris Benedicti, his sacris numismatibus, litteris et characteribus a te designatis, tuam benedictionem infundas, ut omnes qui ea gestaverint ac bonis operibus intenti fuerint, sanitatem mentis et corporis, et gratiam sanctificationis, atque indulgentias nobis concessas consequi mereantur, omnesque diaboli insidias et fraudes, per auxilium misericordiæ tuæ, effugere valeant, et in conspectu tuo sancti et immaculati appareant. Per Dominum nostrum Jesum Christum Filium tuum, qui tecum vivit et regnat in unitate Spiritus Sancti Deus, per omnia sæcula sæculorum.

R. Amen.

OREMUS

Domine Jesu, qui voluisti pro totius mundi redemptione de Virgine nasci, circumcidi, a Judæis reprobari, Judæ osculo tradi, vinculis alligari, flagellis cædi, spinis coronari, clavis perforari, inter latrones crucifigi, lancea vulnerari, et tandem in cruce mori: per hanc tuam sanctissimam Passionem humiliter exoro, ut omnes diabolicas insidias et fraudes expellas ab eo, qui Nomen sanctum tuum his litteris et characteribus a te designatis devote invocaverit, et eum ad salutis portum

perducere digneris, qui vivis et regnas in sæcula
sæculorum.

R. Amen.

Benedictio Dei Patris ✠ omnipotentis, et Filii ✠ et
Spiritus ✠ Sancti descendat super hæc numismata ac
ea gestantes, et maneat semper, in nomine Patris ✠ et
Filii ✠ et Spiritus ✠ Sancti.

R. Amen.

Deinde Sacerdos aspergit numismata aqua benedicta.

CHAPTER XV

ON DEVOTION TO ST. BENEDICT

God has vouchsafed to make choice of his servant Benedict, and to associate the merits of this holy Patriarch with the divine virtue of the sacred cross engraved on the medal which we have described in these pages. This fact seems to require that we should add, in conclusion, a few words, in order to recommend to the faithful a devotion towards so powerful a protector.

The motive for our having a special devotion to any particular saint, is generally based on the merits of that saint, merits which give more than ordinary power to his intercession with God for us. Now, if we consider all that grace has worked in St. Benedict, and all that St. Benedict has done, by himself and by his children, for the honour of God, the salvation of souls, and the service of the Church, we are led to think that amongst the friends of God, and amongst those whom he has mercifully glorified, there are few whose intercession can be more powerful.

That Rule, so holy and so full of wisdom, which for more than five centuries was the only one in all the monasteries of the West! — may we not justly consider it as dictated by the Holy Ghost, to the man who was chosen to write it, and to give it his own name? Those thousands of saints which it has produced, and who gloried in being children of St. Benedict, are they not so many stars which shine in heaven round this bright sun? Whole nations converted from paganism to the Christian faith by his disciples, do they not proclaim him to be their father? The numerous bands of martyrs who honour Benedict with the title of their leader, do they not give him the right to claim a share in the merits of their combats? That almost countless multitude of sainted bishops who have governed so many churches, and that constellation of holy doctors who have taught the sacred sciences and fought against the heresies of their time, do they not also render homage to him whom they all honoured here on earth as their master? The thirty Sovereign Pontiffs whom the Benedictine Rule has given to the Church, and of whom so many were engaged in carrying out measures of the highest importance to the defense and well-being of Christendom, do they not also bear testimony to the deep wisdom of the inspired legislator, under whose guidance they passed so many years in the cloister? In a word, so many millions of souls who have, during the last thirteen hundred years, consecrated themselves to God under the holy and immortal Rule of St. Benedict, do they not form round his venerable head an everlasting crown, which is the admiration of the elect?

All these motives justify every effort which we can make, to persuade Christians, who love to honour those who have been heroes of sanctity, to cultivate a devotion towards the great Patriarch, in whom God seems to have united everything that can give us an idea of the immense glory wherewith he has crowned him in heaven. Let us therefore have recourse to St. Benedict in our necessities; he has power to grant all we ask him; and that wonderfully paternal lovingness which formed quite a leading characteristic of his soul, whilst he was here on earth, (as we learn from the account of his admirable life given us by St. Gregory the Great), that same paternal sweetness is still, now that he is enjoying the happiness of heaven, the peculiarity of his intercession for his clients on earth.[1]

He appeared one day to St. Gertrude, his illustrious daughter. The holy virgin, overwhelmed with admiration at the contemplation of his merits, reminded him of his glorious death, when in the church of Monte Cassino, on the 21st of March 543, after having received the Body and Blood of Our Lord, supported in the arms of his disciples, and standing, as it were, in the attitude of a valiant combatant, he breathed forth his soul to

---

[1] "Give us great hearts, dear Father!—hearts as wide
As thine, that was wider than the world;—
Hearts by incessant labour sanctified,
Yet with the peace of prayer within them furled."—*Faber.*

his God whilst uttering his last prayer. She then ventured to ask him, in the name of his so precious a death, that he would vouchsafe to assist by his presence, at their last moments, each of her Religious who were then living in the convent of which she was abbess. Relying upon the credit which he possessed with the sovereign Lord of all things, the holy Patriarch thus answered her, with that sweet authority which accompanied his words even whilst he was here on earth: "Every one who shall honour me for the privilege wherewith my Divine Master so graciously enriched my death, I promise to be present at his death and assist him. I will be to him as a protection against all those snares which the devils will cruelly lay for him; and comforted by my presence, he shall escape them all, and obtain the bliss of heaven, and there be forever happy."[1]

So consoling a promise made by such a servant of God, and authenticated by such a noble spouse of the Saviour of the world, has inspired the children of St. Benedict with the pious thought of composing a special prayer, in accordance with the intention specified by their Patriarch, in order thus to ensure, to those who recite it, the blessing which he has deigned to promise them. We here give this prayer, with the desire that it may become known and used by the faithful, and secure to them a happy death.

---

[1] S. Gertrudis, Insinuationes Divinæ Pietatis, lib. iv. cap. ii.

ANTIPHON

Benedict, the beloved of Our Lord, whilst standing in the church, having been fortified with the Body and Blood of the Lord, supporting his failing limbs on the arms of his disciples, with his hands upraised to heaven, breathed forth his soul amidst words of prayer, and was seen ascending into heaven by a path most richly hung with tapestry, and lit up with countless lamps.

V. Thou didst appear glorious in the sight of the Lord.

R. *Therefore did he clothe thee with beauty.*

PRAYER

O God! Who didst adorn the precious death of most holy Father

ANTIPHONA

Stans in Oratorio, dilectus Domini Benedictus, Corpore et Sanguine Dominico munitus, inter discipulorum manus imbecillia membra sustentans, erectis in cœlum manibus, inter verba orationis spiritum efflavit, qui per viam stratam palliis, et innumeris coruscam lampadibus, cœlum ascendere visus est.

V. Gloriosus apparuisti in conspectu Domini.

R. *Propterea decorem induit te Dominus.*

ORATIO

Deus, qui pretiosam mortem sanctissimi Patris Benedicti tot tantisque

Benedict, with so many and so great privileges; grant, we beseech thee, that at our death we may be defended from the snares of our enemies, by the blessed presence of him whose memory we celebrate. Through Christ our Lord. *Amen.*

privilegiis decorasti: concede, quæsumus, nobis: ut cujus memoriam recolimus, ejus in obitu nostro beata præsentia ab hostium muniamur insidiis. Per Christum Dominum nostrum. *Amen.*

APPENDIX

APPENDIX

The Centenary Medal Struck At Monte Cassino To Commemorate The 1400th Anniversary Of The Birth Of St. Benedict

Decree of the late Sovereign Pontiff, Pius IX, granting new indulgences to the Centenary Medal

PIUS IX POPE
Unto the perpetual memorial thereof

Whereas the solemn centenary in honour of St. Benedict is to be celebrated in the coming year 1880, whereas also the Crypt in the Arch-Abbey of Monte Cassino, founded by the holy Patriarch himself, and subject to no diocese of our Roman province, and wherein is the tomb of the same St. Benedict and of his sister St. Scholastica, and whereas the tower also in which the Saint himself dwelt in his life on earth are both being restored by means of the offerings of the faithful from

all countries of the world; our beloved son, Nicholaus
d'Orgemont, Abbot Ordinary of Monte Cassino, has, after
wholesome counsel caused the holy and ancient medal
of St. Benedict to be restruck, in order to perpetuate the
memory of that solemnity, and of the piety of the faithful,
and has likewise earnestly besought us to enrich the same
with new indulgences. Wishing with all our heart to
comply with these requests, walking in the footsteps of
our pre-decessors, as a pledge of our special love towards
the above named Arch-Abbey, which, to use the words
of our predecessor Benedict XIII of happy memory, "has
been consecrated by the daily indwelling of its founder
even till his death, and also by the promulgation by him
of his Rule, by the splendour of his miracles, in a word,
ennobled by being the resting place of his sacred body,
and, as fountainhead of the whole Order, has ever been
held in great honour and esteem by all, and especially
by the Roman Pontiffs, our predecessors," trusting in
the mercy of Almighty God, and relying on the authority
of his blessed Apostles SS. Peter and Paul, to each and
all of the faithful of Christ, of both sexes, who shall wear
that holy medal given to them by the Abbot Ordinary
of Monte Cassino for the time being, or by any priest
whom he shall please to delegate for this purpose, to
such as these, by the tenor of these present letters, we
give and grant, besides the indulgences already granted,
power and permission freely and lawfully to gain each
and all the indulgences, plenary as well as partial,
conceded by this Holy See to those visiting the above

named holy places, to wit, the Basilica and Cathedral Church, the Crypt, and Tower of St. Benedict, on condition that they visit some church, or public oratory, and there earnestly pray for the conversion of sinners, and moreover accomplish in the Lord those works of piety usually enjoined. This decree shall hold good, notwithstanding whatsoever may be done contrary to its tenor. For present and future times these letters shall be of effect. We wish, moreover, that to written copies of these presents, or even to printed copies, signed by our public notary, and sealed by the seal of some ecclesiastical dignity, the same weight be given, in all its absoluteness, which would be given to these presents, were they brought forth and shown. Given at Rome, at St. Peter's, under the ring of the Fisherman, on the 31st day of August 1877, in the thirty-second year of our Pontificate.

Signed for his Eminence CARD. ASQUINIO

D. JACOBINI (Substitutus)

A LIST OF SPECIAL INDULGENCES WHICH HAVE BEEN GRANTED BY THE HOLY SEE TO ALL THOSE WHO VISIT THE CATHEDRAL CHURCH OF OUR MOST HOLY FATHER ST. BENEDICT AT THE SAME ABBEY.

I.—For visiting the Basilica or Crypt.

On any day whatever, once in the year:

A *plenary indulgence* to all making a devout pilgrimage to the Arch-abbey of Monte Cassino, granted by Clement XI.

On the Circumcision of our Lord:

An indulgence of two years and two quarantines, granted by Urban V.

On the Epiphany of our Lord and during its octave:

An indulgence of *two years* and *two quarantines,* granted by Urban V.

On the Purification of the B. V. M.:

An indulgence of *five years* and *five quarantines,* granted by Innocent V.

On the Feast of St. Scholastica, Virgin:

A *plenary indulgence,* granted by Urban VII.

An indulgence of *five years* and *five quarantines* during its octave, granted by Innocent VII.

On the Feast of our most Holy Father St. Benedict:

A *plenary indulgence,* granted by Paul V.

An indulgence of *two years* and *two quarantines* during its octave, granted by Urban V.; and also of *one year* and *forty days* during its octave, granted by Alexander IV.

On the Annunciation of the B. V. M.:

An indulgence of *two years* and *two quarantines,* granted by Urban V.

An indulgence of *five years* and *five quarantines,* granted by Innocent VII.

On each of the Sundays of Lent:

An indulgence of *two years* and *two quarantines,* granted by Urban V.

On Easter Sunday and during its octave:

An indulgence of *two years* and *five quarantines,* granted by Innocent VII.

Ascension of Our Lord and during its octave:

An indulgence of *two years* and *two quarantines,* granted by Urban V.

An indulgence of *five years* and *five quarantines,* granted by Innocent VII.

On Whitsunday and the six following days:

An indulgence of *two years* and *two quarantines,* granted by Urban V.

An indulgence of *five years* and *five quarantines,* granted by Innocent VII.

On Corpus Christi and during its Octave:

An indulgence of *two years* and *two quarantines,* granted by Urban V.

On the Feast of the Apostles SS. Peter and Paul:

An indulgence of *two years* and *two quarantines,* granted by Urban V.

On the 2nd of August:

A *plenary indulgence* called of the *Portiuncula,* granted by Pius IX.

On the Assumption of our Blessed Lady:

An indulgence of *two years* and *two quarantines,* granted by Urban V.

An indulgence of *five years* and *five quarantines,* granted by Innocent VII.

On the Feast of the Dedication of the Basilica of Monte Cassino, October 1st:

An indulgence of *forty days,* granted by Alexander II.

An indulgence of *fifty years* and *fifty quarantines,* granted by Benedict XIII.

For visiting the following Altars:

That of our most holy Father St. Benedict in the Crypt, an indulgence of *one hundred days.*

That of the Assumption of the B. V. M., an indulgence of *forty days.*

That of St. John the Baptist, an indulgence of *forty days.*

That of St. Victor, Pope, an indulgence of *forty days:*

all these granted by the consecrators of the altars.

On All Saints and during its Octave:

An indulgence of *two years* and *two quarantines,* granted by Urban V.

On Christmas Day and during its Octave:

An indulgence of *two years* and *two quarantines,* granted by Urban V.

An indulgence of *five years* and *five quarantines,* granted by Innocent VII.

Besides these indulgences, those special indulgences may be gained in the Basilica of Monte Cassino, which Clement X granted to all churches of our Order, viz., a plenary indulgence on the five greater feasts of our Order — on the Feast of our most holy Father St. Benedict, of St. Scholastica, Virgin, of St. Maurus, St. Placid, St. Gertrude, and all Saints of our Order.

II.- For visiting the Tower

in which St. Benedict dwelt during his sojourn on earth, special indulgences are granted.

On each day throughout the year:

An indulgence of *one hundred days,* granted by Gregory XIII.

On the Feast of our most holy Father St. Benedict:

A *plenary indulgence,* granted by Gregory XIII.

On the Feast of the Dedication of the Basilica of Monte Cassino, October 1st:

A *plenary indulgence,* granted by Gregory XIII.

N. B.- These indulgences may be gained by the faithful on the specified days, on their visiting any church or public oratory, provided they wear one of the Monte Cassino Centenary medals blessed by a priest having the power, and fulfill the necessary conditions, according to the decree (Cum Centenaria Solemnia) given above.

EXTRACTS from the LETTER of the Abbot of Monte Cassino "To the Right Rev. Abbots and Prelates Living the Monastic Life" under the Rule of the Great Patriarch St. benedict

.   .   .   .

"The Sovereign Pontiff Pius IX, for the happy success of the works begun in the Arch-Abbey of Monte Cassino, to commemorate the centenary celebration in honour of St. Benedict, in most loving kindness and by autograph letter granted to us, according to our petition, his apostolic benediction, and at the same time was amongst the first, with liberal munificence, to assist us. Moreover, to show the strongest proofs of his Apostolic approbation and benevolence, that most Holy Pontiff willed, in addition to the ordinary indulgences attached to every medal of St.

Benedict, to enrich this one (which we have taken care,
to have struck in a new and more elegant style, in order
to perpetuate the memory of this solemn centenary), with
each and all of those indulgences which may be gained
by visiting the Basilica and Cathedral Church of Monte
Cassino, the Crypt, and also the Tower of our most holy
Father St. Benedict; and these indulgences are granted
to all the faithful for wearing one of the above-mentioned
medals of St. Benedict struck by us, and given to them
by us or by a priest delegated by us."

. . . .

"The faculty of blessing and distributing the medals
of St. Benedict in the new form, enriched with new and
exceptional indulgences, we, by these presents, desire
to communicate to all abbots and prelates serving under
the Rule of our most Holy Father St. Benedict, to whom
also we give power to subdelegate any one they wish
of their own subjects who are both monks and priests.[1]
But it must be borne in mind that this faculty does not
refer to any medal of St. Benedict whatsoever, but only
to those which we have had struck in four sizes, in bronze
and silver, in order to perpetuate the memory of the fourteenth centenary of our most holy Father, and of the so
great and beneficent piety both of his sons and of the
faithful of Christ in general. And without delay, to each
of those monasteries under the Rule of our most holy
Father St. Benedict whose abbots or prelates shall be

[1] Under the current dispensation any priest of the Order of St.
Benedict can bless the medal. —Publishers note.

pleased to make known to us the number of their brethren, together with name and address, we will send gratis,
as many of these medals in bronze as there shall be
brethren in each monastery.

"Moreover, if any one, to increase the devotion and
filial love of the faithful of Christ towards our most holy
Father, wish to obtain more of these medals, let him make
known to us exactly, the size, metal, and number.

THE ENGLISH BENEDICTINE CENTENARY
MEDAL-CROSS.

When God created our first parents and placed them
in the garden of Paradise, he gave them dominion over
the whole world and all that was in it. By their fall they
transferred their allegiance from Him to the devil, who
thereby acquired power over them and their domain; and
from the book of Job and the Gospels, we see what mighty
sway he can wield over man and over all animate and
inanimate nature. Our Blessed Lord came to destroy this
reign of the devil, and He gave to the Apostles, as the
ministers of His Church, power over the devils to cast
them out. The Church directly exercises this power in
blessing the medals of St. Benedict, which are first
exorcised, that is, are withdrawn from the dominion of

the devil, and are blessed and indulgenced, as a protection against temptation, and a preservative against dangers of soul and body.

The Holy See having declared that the blessing and the indulgences attached to the medal may be applied to a medal-cross of St. Benedict, one of a new design has been struck in honour of the fourteenth centenary of St. Benedict's birth, which occurs during this year, 1880.

At the intersection of a floriated Latin cross is placed the medal of St. Benedict. The emblems on the cross recall that heroic act recorded by St. Gregory the Great, when St. Benedict, in the seventeenth year of his age, threw himself into a bed of briars and thistles, to overcome a temptation of the flesh. On the "reverse,' thorns are represented as growing out of the ground, for the senses of man are prone to evil from his youth. In the arms of the cross are placed thistles: besides commemorating St. Benedict's mortification, these deceptive flowers may be regarded as emblems of those sinful pleasures which cannot be indulged in, without their wounding body and soul; "nemo me impune lacessit" has thus a spiritual meaning. Above the medal, in the upper limb of the cross is placed the rose. About seven hundred years after St. Benedict's trial and victory, St. Francis of Assisi visited the spot, and on the briars grafted roses, which are flourishing at the present day.

The rose is placed above the medal, because the thorns and thistles of temptations become flowers of virtue through the prayers and intercession of the Saint.

On the "obverse" of the cross is a lily, the emblem of purity; and, as chastity is a supernatural virtue, it is represented as growing out of a vase, and not out of the earth; and, although the stem is covered with leaves, it only bursts into flower when it surrounds the medal of our holy Father; for the example and protection of the Saints are necessary for the virtue to become perfect and pleasing to God.

HYMN TO ST. BENEDICT

FATHER of many children! in the gloom
  Of the long past, how beautiful thou art!
And still, dear Saint! the weary nations come
  To drink from out thine unexhausted heart.

There are sweet waters in thy fountains still,
  In every changeful age they have been flowing;
While faithful sons thy destinies fulfill
  Through the wide world, like rivers in their going.

Kings with thy wisdom in their hearts, dear Saint!
  Have grown more royal 'neath thy Christlike rule;
And when the earth with ignorance was faint,
  Learning found shelter in thy tranquil school.

Deserts have blossomed where thy feet have trod;
  Thy homes have been safe shelters for the weary;
And in dark times the glory of our God
  Fled to thy houses to find sanctuary.

O Benedict! thy special gifts are peace,
  Freedom of heart and sweet simplicity;
They fail not with the ages, but increase,
  As thine own graces grew of old in thee.

Give us great hearts, dear Father! hearts as wide
    As thine, that was far wider than the world-
Hearts by incessant labour sanctified,
    Yet with the peace of prayer within them furled.

Thou art the Christian Abraham — to thee,
    Saint of insatiate love! thy God hath given,
For thy grand faith, a sainted family,
    Countless as are the crowded stars in heaven.

Kind Shepherd! tend us with thy pastoral love
    Across the mountains to our heavenly rest!
Father! we see thee beckoning from above-
    We come! we come! to bless thee, and be blest!
                                        —*Faber.*

"In all things may God be glorified."
(RULE OF ST. BENEDICT, ch. lvii.)